Gion A. Caminada **on the path
to building**

Gion A. Caminada **on the path to building** A conversation about architecture with Florian Aicher

Birkhäuser
Basel

Editor
Florian Aicher

Printed with financial support from
Pro Helvetia, Schweizer Kulturstiftung
SWISSLOS/Kulturförderung, Kanton Graubünden

Acquisitions Editor: David Marold, Birkhäuser Verlag, A-Vienna
Project and Production Editor: Angelika Heller, Birkhäuser Verlag, A-Vienna
Translation from German into English: Rupert Hebblethwaite, A-Vienna
Cover and typografic concept: Gorbach GmbH, Büro für Gestaltung und Realisierung
Typography: Sven Schrape, D-Berlin
Printing: Holzhausen Druck GmbH, A-Wolkersdorf

Library of Congress Control Number: 2018937219

Bibliographic information published by the German National Library
The German National Library lists this publication in the Deutsche Nationalbibliografie;
detailed bibliographic data are available on the Internet at
http://dnb.dnb.de.

ISBN 978-3-0356-1542-5

German: ISBN 978-3-0356-1540-1

© Images
Aicher, Florian pp. 70, 79, 87, 88, 93, 100, 112, 135; Archiv Vrin p. 52; Caminada, Gion A.
pp. 49, 56, 59, 69, 94, 107, 108, 111, 143, 153, 157, 159.; Degonda, Lucia   pp. 66, 75, 109,
146, 149, 150; Feiner, Ralph pp. 97, 125, 126, 140; Pleps, Hermann p. 103; Steiner, Petra
pp. 17–47, 71, 109, 116, 117, 123, 132, 134, 144; Studio Basel p. 62; Taschen-Verlag p. 118

© 2018 Birkhäuser Verlag GmbH, Basel
P.O. Box 44, 4009 Basel, Switzerland
Part of Walter de Gruyter GmbH, Berlin/Boston

9 8 7 6 5 4 3 2 1   www.birkhauser.com

Inhalt

Home is what is spoken there.

Herta Müller

Introduction

The architect as a communicator of values as exemplified by Gion A. Caminada

This book seeks to characterize Gion Caminada as an architect by exploring his experience of living in Val Lumnezia in the Canton of Graubünden and the influence of this upon his buildings. This is not such an easy task because it requires at least an indication of this experience and his ideals as well as an illustration of how these have informed his work.

My introduction will attempt to be complementary: I will interpret Caminada's work from the perspective of a broadening of architectural theory and practice and, as a result, I hope to underline the added value with which his buildings are imbued.

Both aspects of my argument view this work as an ongoing experiment. Caminada spent his childhood in Vrin, the final village as one climbs Val Lumnezia, where he served an apprenticeship as a carpenter before training as an architect and, finally, becoming a professor at the ETH in Zurich. He lives and works in Vrin to this day. The widespread publication of the design processes and the buildings in Vrin and other places which involved the participation of villagers, foundations, and the authorities have brought Caminada a certain fame in recent years.

An appeal for a different way of practicing architecture

The project in Vrin seems exemplary to me because its notion of designing and building is marked by a close connection between social context, economic conditions, anthropological constants, and historical background. This requires a broadening of the notion of architecture and regional planning because only this will make it possible to have a real conversation with the affected inhabitants and to include their problems in the planning process with due care and attention.

The thing about Caminada that particularly impresses me is his understanding of the architect's role as a communicator of values that he seeks to render visible, values of which we may well be still aware but which are often set aside during the building process, or values that do not even feature in the teaching and training of today. Participative building, as practiced by Caminada, demands strategies that are coupled with the creation of sustainable meaning. As soon as people are able to recognize that their interests are being taken seriously and that they, too, can participate in the discussion of these various issues, the identity of a village community is strengthened and communication amongst these people intensifies. This can all be seen and learned in Vrin.

A further important aspect of Caminada's exemplary work is his attempt to reacquaint the community with disappearing rituals and time-honored customs. An example of this is his mortuary in Vrin. The fact that people are dying more and more frequently in hospitals or old people's homes means that laying out at home is no longer customary, even in the valleys of the Alps. The rites of passage before the funeral that were practiced in earlier times are now possible again in this mortuary in which the coffin is laid out in an intimate, "warm atmosphere."

The method of knitted construction that is used on both the exterior and the interior of the building contributes to the sense of well-being within the space. It almost feels like a parlor. The mood of the lighting can be regulated by the shutter to the window behind the laid out body.

The human yearning to feel "protected" by architecture is taken very seriously by Caminada. At the Girls' Dormitory in Disentis he selected a concept in which he treated the inner core, which consists of a stair and an associated "vestibule," as a communication space. The stair spirals upwards at every level so that each "vestibule" is positioned on a different façade. Within the circulation core he uses the niches under the stairs as intimate places of retreat. In this way he responds to the human desire for protected spaces, for the "warmth of the nest" that should always be incorporated into the design, regardless of whom it is for.

In addition to this he varies the depths of the windows in the wall. A typical feature of his work, this creates niches that are visible from both within and without and can be used as places for sitting or lying.

The perceptual and psychological aspects of the auras of internal and external spaces are another central theme in Caminada's work. He justifiably refers to the positive or negative impact on people's behavior of the atmosphere of architecture and spaces. By creating spatial effects that also make use of acoustic and olfactory characteristics he consciously seeks to positively manage well-being and behavior. I find it extraordinary not only that an architect can dispose of so much knowledge drawn from so many areas of expertise but also that he can bring this expertise to life through his building, his counseling, his teaching, and, thus, his exemplary demonstration of how communities can be positively influenced. In this sense, Caminada is playing a role that no longer features in the job description of the architect: the role of an architectural or planning therapist or, indeed, of a mentor.

The meaning of materials and aesthetic in Caminada's work

If one looks carefully one sees that Caminada's attitude is closely related to his journey through life. His experience of his home village was extremely positive and he established himself there, as a carpenter and, later, as an architect. This gave him the ideal tools for making the village attractive again to its inhabitants. An example: He is aware of the positive effect on people of the gentle aromas of certain species of wood, as demonstrated in his "Tegia da vaut" forest hut in Domas-Ems. This is a meeting place for people learning a number of forest-related professions. The hut sits in a forest clearing, integrated into nature. As a result of the management of the light and the choice of materials the hut radiates an atmosphere that is shaped by perceptible factors.

In his work, Caminada shows us many ways of using wood. He repeatedly returns to his beloved knitted construction, which is based on the use of solid wooden logs, and combines this traditional building method with many of his own inventions and variations which stretch to the use of forgotten materials and techniques such as the basket weaving that he uses in the stair of the viewing tower in Reussdelta. Caminada's deep interest in the need for intimacy and comfort can be seen in the dining rooms of his restaurants and his hotel rooms. These are tailored to the human scale, places in which one feels good and at ease. This added value that is generated by the mobilization of the senses comes about because he translates his knowledge of our fundamental psychological needs into designs of high aesthetic quality.

It is no coincidence that over the course of the past few years the multi-purpose hall in Vrin with the wonderful roof structure – with ties made from anchored tensile timber straps designed by the engineer Jürg Conzett – has joined Peter Zumthor's thermal baths in Vals as one of the most published buildings of the 'Graubünden School'. Caminada's many buildings, even such simple ones as the barns at Sut Vitg, the small mortuary or the Alig carpentry workshop in Vrin, meet the highest aesthetic expectations in terms of architecture and interior design.

Caminada combines many astonishing qualities. Whether judged on its social, anthropological, perceptual/ psychological, constructive or aesthetic aspects his work is regarded as culturally sophisticated and exemplary.

The contribution of Caminada's work to the theory of regionalism

"Distance breeds indifference ... for the individual must feel responsible for the whole" is one of Caminada's favorite quotes. For him, this represents a partial but in no way a total rejection of the globalization that is practiced today around the world. Because even the regional requires this sense of the whole. He himself makes use of the achievements of new technologies insofar as these serve the further development of human capabilities and are not weighed down by too many side-effects. Here, Caminada takes up the ideas of "Critical Regionalism" of the architectural historian Kenneth Frampton and the philosopher Paul Ricœur. These illustrate how a hybrid global culture can only emerge out of cross-fertilization between solidly rooted and universal cultures. For Ricœur, everything depends upon the capacity of regional cultures to absorb traditions while remaining open to influences from global cultural movements. Caminada also knows how tradition and process can be combined in order to contribute to the development of the process of civilization.

As he commented: "Neither tradition nor modernity, we are seeking a situation that allows us to escape these alternatives: This can only be the here and now."

The Vrin project is merely the start

Having originated as a private initiative and been widely disseminated by the media, the Vrin project has been followed very carefully by politicians, sociologists, planners, and agricultural economists.

But rather than being finished, Caminada prefers to see it as one of his life-long tasks. He claims that everything is constantly "in a state of flux" as a result of which he doesn't see his interventions in Vrin as a project, because projects have a beginning and an end. It is being followed up at ETH Zurich because Caminada has been a professor of architecture and design there for many years, a position that he has used in order to convince young people of the above-mentioned fundamentals of architecture and regional planning as well as to involve them in the design process on the ground. As Caminada says, "the objective is to learn for other places."

Francois Burkhardt,
Berlin, December 2017/January 2018

Caminada's paths

An illustrated essay
by Petra Steiner

43

Cons

So it happened again the night before last: The fox grabbed — well — not a goose but a couple of chickens instead. Such incidents are part of life up here. It was the neighbor who was affected. Things like this have become less common – people say that these wild animals are no longer part of our culture and you don't expect to see them. Earlier we protected the chickens from the fox as a matter of course. Today we simply shoot him and other animals, eliminate the things that make our life less comfortable. But this unconditional mastery over nature isn't working. We have to learn again: how to deal with the unexpected, to care for our home, to protect our domestic animals.

Cons: at the far end of Val Lumnezia, below Pitz Terri (3,149 m), and at the foot of the pass over the Greina.

The unexpected

It's exactly the same in other areas. Just consider – for example – what we invest in barriers against avalanches, in protecting buildings, and then in providing access – one after the other. Often it would be more logical not to open up every last bit of land. Natural events can't be foreseen with complete certainty. They occur just when you're not expecting them. Uncertainty is ever present – we know that up here. We'll never gain complete control. **That's part of what one learns from having to deal with such things. And conversely, learning to deal with such things is the best way of reacting to – and, to a certain extent, controlling – the unforeseeable.** If we deal with them, we understand them, appreciate them – they become part of our lives. Today, however, we often see them as no more than objects that we have at our command. Ideally, the fox is dead and the slope that is prone to avalanches is covered with concrete. But our lives would be richer if we saw these as living things. **That's how life was up here: we let things be.** And yet: This approach is disappearing. Things could also be different. In his novel "Terror on the Mountain" Charles Ferdinand Ramuz writes that the mountains have their own will because they have their own plan.[1] Maybe the mountains do have their own will ... when I was young nature was neither good nor evil – it was what it was. Today everything seems to be predictable. Technical progress gives us the impression that there's nothing that can't be calculated. It's not enough for us today that something is simply there; we're constantly seeking to decide and determine how it should be ... And yet we've achieved so much technically that culture and nature could have a completely different relationship. I'm not remotely arguing for a return to animism, to some obscure means of giving souls to objects. But the way that we act today, always regarding the world as no more than a resource, a commodity, a consumer article, is stupid and arrogant. I remember when things were different. When the relationship between farmers and nature was instant and direct. But even if we can't return

---

[1] Ramuz, Charles Ferdinand: Terror on the Mountain, transl. by Milton Stansbury, Harcourt, Brace & World, New York 1967.

to those times we need to rediscover something of this interdependency between nature and people. In my projects I try to overcome this separation between culture and nature – to deny that these are alternatives.

In motion

You grew up here, with people and animals and buildings and mountains and the weather. Rural life brought you into contact with all of this ... and also gave our life a certain rhythm. A typical example of our form of cultivation was terrace farming, which meant that there was room for everything. Everything had its time, its special place, was subject to events. It was a lean existence, formative and unequivocal! It was the way that it was! Not otherwise! **Terrace farming – how should one visualize that?** The different levels at which the cattle are kept are cultivated in different ways depending upon the climate, the condition of the soil, and the vegetation. On the valley floor: the farmhouse and the barn – where we live, this level is already well above the very bottom of the valley. Then the middle level which, unlike the valley floor, only produced a single hay harvest. This is where the cows grazed, were herded, and spent the night in the barn while we returned to the village in the evening before returning uphill the next morning. In summer the farmers drove the cattle to the upper pastures where there were communal herdsmen and dairymen. Up there wild hay was grown – and only harvested every second year. **The area around Vrin which, after all, is situated at 1,450 meters above sea level, is bright and sunny, particularly on this side of the valley; how did this form of cultivation shape the landscape?** Every piece of viable land was put to use and the pastures and the meadows pushed back the forest over the centuries.

How did one move around such a widespread area? The cattle set the tone. They were driven out to grass and the people followed, leaving for the pastures and the meadows in the morning to find the cattle and returning to the village in the evening. **Tremendous distances!** And all on foot. As a lad I had to look after the animals on the *Maiensäss*, the pastures halfway up the mountains, in spring – before they were driven up onto the higher pastures in summer – and in au-

Just two generations ago: A patchwork of small fields shapes the landscape around Cons.

tumn on their return. Considerable distances, every day, often more than an hour, narrow paths. My mother packed the rucksack. Landjäger had just appeared – a new sausage, produced more or less industrially – every day I got a half. That was all we could afford. No one had much money. Halfway up the mountain I'd already eaten half of this half a Landjäger. By the time I arrived, my father had already milked the cows so I let them out of the barn. We worked from sunrise to sunset. At the end of the day I was happy when the cattle returned to the stall and I could go home – how long some of those days seemed to last if there weren't any other boys around to play with! Looking after the cattle was boys' work. There was a lot going on on those pastures; each farming family looked after their own animals – they only wanted the best for them. I hardly ever got up to the high summer pastures because, as the only son, I had to help at home with the haymaking and other things. Down in the valley and halfway up the mountain the hay was kept in barns; in those days you brought the cattle to the barn but now you bring the hay to the cattle. **A busy way of life. Also because**

the land was so widely dispersed, a patchwork of small plots.
Yes, there were meadows here and there, up above and down
below. We knew them all individually, each had a different
meaning, different characteristics – things grew differently
here, the hay dried differently there. This knowledge was of
existential importance. Each meadow had a name which
reflected these concrete characteristics.

Changes

**It goes without saying that the weather and the seasons had a
major impact. Most of the time the cattle were outside. So what
did you do in winter?** The snow was a real burden. The farmers stayed with the cattle on the upper pastures until Christmas.
They worked in the barn between five and eight in the morning,
returned to the village, did things, went back up the mountain
after two, worked in the barn again till six. And then they slept
in the barn. We stayed in the village between January and May,
the cattle were in the valley, too, then started back up the mountain in May, first to the *Maiensäss*, then to the *Alp*, the upper
pasture. But now and again we had to climb the mountain in
winter too, to collect the wild hay from the highest pasture, tie
it into bundles and drag it down on the frozen snow. Otherwise
we stayed at home and kept busy. But when the days got longer
it was high time to move outside. **How did you deal with the
weather in general?** We kept an eye on the weather, tried to
interpret it, planned our day accordingly. This worked pretty
well. It was as if the weather was made here, although of course
one couldn't really make the weather, not even back then. Some
people just knew: When that cloud up there is floating like
that then this is going to happen – watch and feel. We had to
pay more attention to all of these things. Predictions based on

senses and the emotions. Because weather's very local. We didn't watch the aesthetically elaborate signs on the horizon like the visitors from the city. And if we did, then these signs meant something favorable or threatening to our very existence. Back then in the valley: The world, time, and space were as one.

Things

Clouds, animals, plants, landscapes – things that are ever present; they all create work. As do the house, the barn, the machinery. According to Martin Heidegger it's such things that create places that bring space, man, and time together.[2]   A place is a location where something happens. A location is, in itself, still nothing. It becomes a place when it becomes a collection of buildings and people and, equally formative, of emotions, moods, events, coincidences ... the places, the landscape: This is still farmland, created by farmers. But today I rarely see farmers, mechanization has put paid to this activity.   **You still directly experienced this continuity of space and time.**   And it was an exciting continuity – time, for example, had its rhythms. The 20th of May and the 20th of September when the cattle left the barn or returned from the high pastures were real highlights. At the end of a long winter this day in May was particularly special. Bells were hung around the cows' necks and the whole valley suddenly began to chime.   **This continuity of space, of time, was very concrete, not at all abstract.**   Life here was defined by this sense of completeness, I still miss it a little. There wasn't this radical division into people, nature, animal, mineral that we have today ... The day was a holistic entity of

---

2   Heidegger, Martin: Building Dwelling Thinking, in: Poetry, Language, Thought, transl. by Albert Hofstadter, Harper Colophon, New York, 1971.

space and time. In my projects I try to work with today's tools to reunite things that have become divided over the years. **The daily routines, the work that had to be done, were decisive.** The most pressing matters set the agenda – life was never just about the present, but it was also as if the distant past and the far-off future didn't exist, just the hope that one day things would be better, easier. One hoped for better times.

Place and spirit
The social aspect was a perfectly natural part of this interaction. The interdependencies were so strong that there was no other option – this was an obligation, a form of pact. Trusting each other and depending upon each other in equal measure. Back then you were always running into someone. Today you only find people up here in the pastures at certain times. Not, however, that there was anything romantic or idyllic about these interactions, because when one's part of an event there's nothing romantic about it; one's involved rather than standing on the sidelines. **So you directly experienced this merging of space, time, and society. One can draw an analogy with contemporary scientific ideas about human thought. The neurologist Ernst Pöppel put it as follows: "As a result of the high level of interconnectedness of the brain no perceptive act is independent of an emotional evaluation or free from a reference to our memories. Everything act of seeing, every image is immersed in our emotional universe, our past, and our memories as well our future intentions."[3]** Today that might just be theory, but I was

---

3 Pöppel, Ernst: Der Rahmen, dtv, Munich 2010, p. 152, transl. by R.H. Ernst Pöppel, *1940, Emeritus Professor of Medical Psychology at the LMU Munich, is one of Germany's leading neurological researchers. Member of the National and European Academies of Sciences and Arts.

able to feel and experience it – to the benefit of my current work. **Places and events that last mere seconds merge into images; and these form the basis of episodic memory. According to Pöppel this is the core of the personal identity.** That would be the world of the senses and the intellect. But I wonder: Does this also contain the non-concrete world, the designs and projects that are so important to us architects, everything which has yet to exist? Which is beyond memory, which is new – but which maybe isn't so new after all? Could it be that the new is simply a reconnection, a rearrangement of these earlier episodes?

Massive parallelism
Today's neurologists have a remarkable view of the way in which the mind works. Ernst Pöppel regards this process as something unique. It isn't a linear series of steps as in a computer but an explosive expansion and an intense gathering of stimuli – thousands of reactions to each stimulus. He refers to this as "massive parallelism".[4] I see a massif, like a block of granite that displays no clear lines, a body that perceives, that has experienced, a bearer of resources and impulses. Not dead, but capable of being reinvigorated, of

A boulder lying in a field.

resonating. **Resonance: the vibration of a body in response to the vibration of another body in a system capable of resonance. Or, as Goethe put it: "Relationship, life is a relationship," which logically implies: "No living thing is One, I say, But always**

---

4   Pöppel, Ernst: Der Rahmen, dtv, Munich 2010, p. 112.

Many."[5] Is that the Vrin experience? Or is that your experience?
You can put it like that. But rather than emerging serenely this
One imposes itself upon you. It leads to dependencies that
grow in importance and become relationships. And you react
by setting things in motion at your end. Is the mountain any
different from the city in this way? Up here, in this apparently
small world, there's certainly more pressure on me to make
something of it. Understanding – and surviving in – this small
world is a complex task. If I'm to create something I have to
concentrate a lot more, do more of the thinking myself. I have
to get involved up here because escape, diversion, evasion isn't
an option! But this forced concentration brings me further!
Here I remain confronted, sometimes to the extent that I begin
to suffer ... But, as we know: When we're designing we can
suffer "like a pig" and yet there are moments when such suffering is essential if we want to make progress because this can
lead to passion, and then deliverance in the form of an idea.
But will this idea stand up to inspection? I could just abandon
it and keep going – but no, that doesn't work. Only by per-
sisting can I be absolutely certain. And then am I right? Beckett already knew: "All of old. Nothing else ever. Ever tried.
Ever failed."[6] His conclusion: "Fail better." That doesn't have
to be our conclusion.   **But maybe it describes how intensity
emerges. The world up here has demanded that of you – and**

---

5   Goethe, Johann Wolfgang von: Zwei poetische Merksprüche, in: Geulen Eva, Aus dem
    Leben der Form, August Verlag, Berlin 2016, p. 58 (Epirrhema: You must, when con-
    templating nature, Attend to this, in each and every feature; there's nought outside and
    nought within, For she is inside out and outside in, Thus will you grasp, with no delay,
    The holy secret, clear as day. Joy in semblance take, in any Earnest play: No living thing
    is One, I say, But always Many. Transl. from Bell, Matthew, (ed.): The Essential Goethe,
    Princeton University Press, Princeton, 2016, p. 29).

6   Beckett, Samuel: Worstward Ho, John Calder, London 1983, p. 7.

has offered you diversity and abundance – and few distractions.
We didn't take those countless paths every day of our own free
will. The farmer knew nothing of hiking and rambling, he
wouldn't have dreamed of climbing the mountain if he didn't
have to. Neither did he have the time. And yet we really had to
walk those distances, not just think about doing so. How we
were amazed by the tourists when they started coming. The
farmer must achieve the goal that he sets himself – the tourist
merely wants to. And because the farmer doesn't see the difference between intention and execution, he's unaware of
the idyllic and the romantic. His relationship with the world
around him is direct. I see this as a different relationship – not
necessarily a better one.

Paths
**The farmers up here didn't have an image of the mountains,
they simply moved amongst them. Paths, all the time, everywhere. Paths bring the distant object closer, in terms of both
space and time, past and future. Taking the same path is a
recurring action and yet is never the same.** That's always the
case up here. The path is a challenge, it demands something
of the body, but it doesn't confront. It creates reality. One sets
off, taking this path or that one, without ever knowing exactly
where it will lead. Something happens, something is added
and then I have something else. Which is also wonderful. How
can I use this today? I'm so grateful that I was able to enjoy
this experience, to sense this form of spatial proximity, of time
being stretched. As Eduardo Chillida says, it's the character
of things that matter rather than their image. **That was well
put. And then there's the name. This establishes what happened,
ascertains what moves, what was present. The word takes**

precedence over the actual occurrence, threatens to conceal it. There are hints of rigidity, allegation, principle, and dogma. **Bruno Latour says: "The word has gone from being a conduit to being an obstacle."[7]** I distance myself from things, suggest something about them, and say: That's the truth. From close range it's completely different. Here, things are so ambiguous that you can't say anything definitive. **And if I'm in motion a thing has many sides.** And the movement itself is also different – I myself, space, time are all in motion. I can take the same path a thousand times and each time it's different. This was the case with my paths, the paths taken by the farmers' lad: always the same, always different. That was a world of its own. **For Bruno Latour it's presence that counts: "It's more a matter of understanding anew, based on present experience, what the tradition might well be able to say, lending us as it then does the words, the same words, but said differently. We don't have to innovate, but to *represent* the same."[8]** We understand the traditional today thanks to the old words of the tradition as we use them here and now. "Episodes of closeness are regrouped to form a quite different story, which flows back from that first time today to all the other times, going back, through

Paths.

a retroactive movement, from the present to the past and to the

7   Latour, Bruno: Rejoicing: Or the Torments of Religious Speech, transl. by Julie Rose, Polity Press, Cambridge 2013, p. 76. Bruno Latour, *1947, sociologist and philosopher, teaches in Paris and knows "that *matters of fact* are poor substitutes for experience." B.L.: Elend der Kritik, Diaphanes, Zurich/Berlin 2007, p. 52.

8   Latour, Bruno: Rejoicing: Or the Torments of Religious Speech, transl. by Julie Rose, Polity Press, Cambridge 2013, p. 72.

time to be."⁹ Rather than being the sequence of past, present, and future, time starts now. A few days ago I had a formative experience. I had the opportunity to join a guided tour of Strasbourg Cathedral and I asked myself: Why don't we still have things like this today? There are many possible answers but what occurred to me was that: Our life in the here and now isn't intense enough. Either we romanticize the past or we're enthralled by visions of the future. We've lost our confidence and trust in the present. But which present? Isn't this no more than a shimmering window, disconnected from life, isolated from the physical passage of time? If this is the case then the present renders us helpless. Those farmers' paths were completely different – we knew: What is, happens. **An intense here and now – where the past doesn't freeze, the present doesn't flow on by, the future isn't just a huge promise. Latour counters such pathos: "Tradition finds itself effectively revived, twisted askew to get it to bring forth the present once more."¹⁰** If I define tradition as that which is proven, then my starting point is that which I use today. The proven has as much to do with the present as with the past. It enables us to trust in the present. And: without such trust nothing can prove itself. When one has trust one can stay alert, watch carefully, remain open. This becomes especially important in view of the huge outside forces affecting us today – the obvious is no longer enough. This obliges us to reflect very carefully. We've wandered from the path, our earlier self-confidence has worn thin, 'keep on going' is no longer an option. I have to deal with these

9 Latour, Bruno: Rejoicing: Or the Torments of Religious Speech, transl. by Julie Rose, Polity Press, Cambridge 2013, p. 52.

10 Latour, Bruno: Rejoicing: Or the Torments of Religious Speech, transl. by Julie Rose, Polity Press, Cambridge 2013, p. 77.

outside forces, whether they are destructive or constructive. We need attention and self-awareness. We have to take decisions – this lies at the heart of every culture.

Difference

Imagination alone isn't enough, you have to do it. You have to set off along the path. That's how it was. But a lot has changed, machines, tools arrived that made life easier. We're glad to have them. It's strange how long it took us to escape from the old direct approach; when we had to climb a steep slope with the sickle bar we still pushed hard – we wanted to help the machine. Later, powerful, sophisticated machines appeared and we learnt to control them. But whether agriculture up here will ever be computerized? ... How direct these earlier experiences were in comparison with the circuitry of today's world! I experience difference by examining the traces of these two worlds. And I can translate this into quality of life. The new world is extremely important because otherwise I would have remained back there, standing still. But I'm also thankful to the old one for teaching me to react. Today, the people up here are also exposed to the outside world, the world has reached Vrin. Problems arise when one can't appreciate the difference or, worse still, when one thinks that only one world should count. The loss of the other would be devastating."[11] A landscape and a culture like we have up here react to new influences with great sensitivity. We have to develop this into a deeper, autonomous culture. But can we?

11 Heidegger, Martin: Discourse on Thinking, transl. by John M. Anderson and Hans Freund, Harper & Row, New York, Evanston and London 1966, p. 54.

Simultaneous

Is that the challenge: to live with both these ways of seeing the world? Yes – to make a whole out of them, or at least to ensure that they tolerate each other as they exist side by side. Neither can claim to be completely in the right. **To understand the rural, the agricultural, as a valuable contribution to the urban market in ideas and services?** The major study of Switzerland carried out by the ETH Studio Basel[12] ten years ago succinctly presented two alternatives: here, the city, in which money talks and there, the mountains, which aren't financially viable. This is more than questionable. The city should acknowledge its dependency upon the countryside and, conversely, the mountains must see themselves as more than just a leisure facility. Ramuz wrote that the mountain is beautiful but that it isn't our friend.[13] Such is the severity of the

"Alpine wasteland – zones of decline and depletion". In: "Switzerland: An urban portrait", 2006.

economic perspective that seeks to overshadow everything. Switzerland's great quality is that all these differences exist in such a small space. This is why I demand that the development of the countryside and the mountains must go hand in hand with that of the cities. We're well aware of the fact that the mountain environment is no longer just an agricultural environment. And this means that we must readdress the role of our mountain regions – also within Switzerland. According to today's dominant economic

---

12 ETH Studio Basel: Switzerland. An urban portrait, 3rd Volume, Basel 2006.

13 Ramuz, Charles Ferdinand: Terror on the Mountain, transl. by Milton Stansbury, Harcourt, Brace & World, New York 1925.

approach such mountain regions have all but lost their *raison d'être*, but we can't deal with them with reason and economic thinking alone. We must not only reconcile the natural elements with modern ways of life and economic systems but also reinforce the differences. Differences emerge as a result of not only the subjective will but also the proximity of things and the understanding of external and internal realities. The mountain needs the city and the city needs the mountain, its resources and its potential. **Reducing resources to the issue of their utilization is extremely short-sighted; because potential is also that which isn't yet here.** It isn't only that which it isn't yet here, it has to be seen and made, through being valued, through being appreciated. It's no help at all when someone from the city comes up the mountain, bringing all his images, data, and algorithms with him. When I occasionally escape from the daily grind and climb to the very head of the valley it's quite empty – empty of people, too. And suddenly it's there: the energy. This is completely different from the office where I feel as if I'm at the center of everything and everything is under control. At the head of the valley this means nothing; I feel how tiny I am or, put another way, how unimportant: which of course means, conversely, how important, how magnificent everything is out here. Suddenly: I experience the world. Sublime. Beautiful. The potential is huge. And far more than all these theme parks or 'experiential worlds' – this is a truly experiential space. You climb up here, on foot, you feel your legs, feel yourself, the mountain, everything around you, and not for a brief moment but for a while – a feeling of such intensity! **A certain non-calculable potential: It's now a decade since Studio Basel and you've been teaching at ETH Zurich since about 2000. A lot's changed in this time. Does the urban**

63

lifestyle still generate the same euphoria that it did ten years ago? Cracks are beginning to show. Do we know how the city is changing? Do we know how the mountains are changing? We're living in the here and now but we must keep searching, not allow ourselves to be bought off with simplistic theories. We won't solve everything, and neither do we have to, but we must keep working away. This is an attitude that I've learnt up here. To be contemporary rather than modern, as Nietzsche demanded! If I'm contemporary – I belong to the place, participate, rather than watching from the sidelines. In contrast with the modern, design, style – if I'm a modern architect I'm already too late. Modernity is a curse. As Nietzsche concluded, only the outmoded can be modern.[14]

Global
Studio Basel's study largely accepted the hardly overwhelming theory that there is a global social trend towards major cities and urban lifestyles. The antithesis, the provincial, belongs to the dustbin of history. Of course one can see this otherwise. Bruno Latour, at any rate, recently stated that "it's perhaps hard to believe but Europe has succeeded in safeguarding its rural areas, its landscapes."[15] He sees this as a significant advantage for a future Europe that is clearly under threat from its own abstraction. "Europe's greatest crime was to be taken in by the belief that it could simply impose itself upon places, regions, countries, and cultures ... and break with the past."[16] And he responds by writing that "this is exactly what we need:

14 Nietzsche, Friedrich: Unzeitgemäße Betrachtungen, ed. by Giorgio Colli and Mazzino Montinari, Vol. 1. Munich 1999, p. 247.
15 Latour, Bruno: FAZ 7.10.2017, No. 233, p. L7, transl. by R.H.
16 Latour, Bruno: FAZ 7.10.2017, No. 233, p. L7, transl. by R.H.

a local, indeed, a provincial experiment, as a means of finding out what it means to inhabit a world after modernization."[17] **Europe is predestined to play this role, is in a position to "deglobalize" globalization.** In anthropological terms, the global is overestimated. All meanings evolve locally – every love affair requires proximity. That which is important to me emerges from a conversation. Of course people travel, listen to music from all over the world, and get excited by every sort of distant deity – and what chaos ensues! But this only makes it even clearer to me that the decisive things happen locally, that it's here that we find what we need. **Which is in itself a universal theory that, more precisely, states that: Local essentially means different. That would be Latour's Europe: one of differences. It is these that should be strengthened if we want to ensure a world of diversity and richness.** My work with differences tells me that if I want to be able to act at all a situation must be manageable. I must work within boundaries. How can I accept responsibility for the entire world? How can I establish a point of view when my context is infinite? I focus on the specific because then I know where the wind is coming from and can sense the other influences. And, conversely, I also know the consequences of my actions elsewhere when I do something foolish here. Earlier, we were less aware of this. **One's own point of view, which also establishes one's identity, is generated by boundaries – and, vice-versa: Without identity there can be no boundaries. As Heidegger observed in his lecture on building "A boundary is not that at which something stops but ... from which something *begins***

---

17   Latour, Bruno: FAZ 7.10.2017, No. 233, p. L7, transl. by R.H.

its presencing."[18]   Latour's words are pretty amazing. The talk is of nations, of the fatherland, of land that should become the fatherland. This is the context of Heidegger's "new down-to-

"Stiva da morts" Mortuary, 2003.
A space from wood, stone, plaster.

earthness" which emerges from his openness and his nonchalant approach to things. Identity and difference – both count, as long as we don't overdo it and simply leave things and people in peace. ... Such observations were decisive in the Mortuary: There, it wasn't about the individual: it was about involving everyone: every person, not personality. Becoming part of the process, the grief, the farewell, the final journey. This worked pretty well there. The Mortuary lives.

Local

Does that work everywhere?   Alexander Kluge[19] speaks on one occasion about the world as a village, characterized by the "predominance of the intimate." That was once the case, but has it vanished? He continues: "The principle of the village or the intimate has disintegrated from an all-powerful present into the elements of a lost past and a hope for the future." So where is it now? It's still here. "Now we carry the principle of the village within us," says Kluge.   **At any rate you regarded**

18 Heidegger, Martin: Building Dwelling Thinking, in: Poetry, Language, Thought, transl. by Albert Hofstadter, Harper Colophon, New York 1971, p. 154. Heidegger's 1951 lecture at the "Darmstädter Gespräche" Symposium under the chairmanship of Otto Bartning and with the participation of some of post-war Germany's most outstanding architects.

19 Kluge, Alexander: Der Angriff der Gegenwart auf die übrige Zeit, Syndikat/EVA, Frankfurt am Main 1985, p. 28, transl. by R.H. Alexander Kluge, *1932, Lawyer, studied under Th. W. Adorno, writer and influential representative of new German cinema.

the preference for the city as arrogant.   And I fight it. Anyone who seeks to make decisions about Switzerland must allow for, involve, develop the edges, the periphery.   **An image of collapse: here the bustling cities, there the mountains, foxes, and bears – an image, a cliché. A contrast in which difference has become distance. Whereas it should be a question of interaction.** The difficulty is: How does such a relationship come about? That was an important issue at the Adula National Park. The city dwellers wanted an oasis and conservation; the mountain dwellers were afraid of restrictions. The project was plagued by misunderstandings. We have to find a new balance. How can we bring these different perspectives together in such a way that a new form of cultural landscape can emerge? One in which differences can lead to a common solution. The main question can't be what is possible? but, rather, what do we want? It can't be right that people come from the city and pay a fortune for barns that were worth no more than a few cents to the farmers – this destroys any equilibrium between the landscape and society. My conclusion is that we need a new equilibrium that maintains the tension in the cultural landscape that's certainly lost if every barn becomes a weekend home for city dwellers. Because when that happens the world for which the tourist so desperately longs is also lost.   **So there will be new differences, but a thread must remain stretched between them – a thread which remains under tension but mustn't be allowed to break.**   When characteristics, new or old, are related, such tensions are generated. This can be positive, and differences can be triggered.

Almens

As Martin Heidegger put it, places emerge from things, from "the nature of the things that are locations and that we call buildings."[20] The nature of buildings is dwelling, which is much more than merely inhabiting. This is particularly important when creating new buildings on the edge of functioning settlements. How does a place become a residential location that is suitable for dwelling? On the edge of Almens you're designing such a place – around 25 residential units, primarily collective, for families with children, developed by a residents' association with which you've been working for a year. What was the key? The client's initial desire was to find an alternative to the single-family house. As most people covet the single-family house we understood our task as follows: to discover the essence of such a form of living, recognize its qualities, and record its deficits. The outcome: A compact development of single-family houses – dense and free at the same time.

The new village
You're achieving this by combining the buildings, three and four-story residential blocks, into two groups of three; separated by a spatial zone which you call the purpose-free space. Covered by a roof and protected, but still outside. This purpose-free space, which almost completely surrounds the actual residential core, offers a sort of "large-scale freedom." On the one hand this is quite normal, on the other hand spatially new. A space that, in geometrical and functional terms, isn't fully

---

20 Heidegger, Martin: Building Dwelling Thinking, in: Poetry, Language, Thought, transl. by Albert Hofstadter, Harper Colophon, New York 1971, p. 158.

defined, that should encompass all possibilities. The whole becomes heterotypical, as opposed to being functionally determined, unambiguous. And because it's so normal special things can happen. **Like the single-family house?** Yes, like the sense of living in a single-family house surrounded by a meadow. People want that. It's a good thing, the individual house, one's own, one's property. Too much

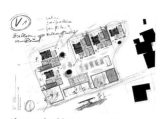

Almens: buildings with external spaces and a shared free space.

property can get in the way of living together but too little can lead to a sense of indifference. Boundaries become important; we have to set boundaries or, better said, markers. This may sound indelicate – but we need them, they define our own space and respond to our own needs, permit encounters with neighbors. Here, these are the shared walls and floors between the apartments. Boundaries are fundamental; the way we deal with them, with their ambiguity, is fascinating. They create a sense of something different. Boundaries enable culture to emerge; culture can establish boundaries. Boundaries can be something very special; making the comparison with biological cells Alexander Kluge says: "If the cell could speak it would say that I permit entry and I form a boundary."[21] Spatial quality is also determined by boundaries. **First and foremost, these spatial boundaries permit intimate spaces, privacy. Not like most of today's developments where neighbors can look into each other's kitchens and which are surrounded by lawns.** We concentrated this outside space and protected it, pushed

21 Von Schirach, Ferdinand und Kluge, Alexander: Die Herzlichkeit der Vernunft, Luchterhand, Munich 2017, p. 150, transl. by R.H.

the "houses" together in order to create a lot of space, new space. Of course this is public space, but I prefer the term free space. In a public space one expects something to happen, but not in a free space, this is more open – even to chance.

Learning from the village

Here I'm making use of my experience of Vrin where the transitions between private, semi-public, and public are completely informal. The square in front of the church is clear – as is the private garden. But how does one order the narrow street in front of the house, which is sometimes an area of grass, or the alley between two buildings? These are transitional spaces that have little to do with regulated town planning. Here, habits, conventions, and practice are as effective as concrete things – whether these are fences or chicken coops. Buildings which touch and roofs which overlap are equally effective – there is a constant transition between density and distance and yet everyone knows: This is mine and that is public. We also

External spaces in the village: asphalted road, gravel path, footpath, public green space, private garden, terraces – a hierarchy of spaces, informal.

made use of such interrelationships, which become recognizable in our built forms, in the dialogue between volumes and roofs. This is a reference to the way in which the old village is built. ... You have to take care not to overdo it. But you can continue the game using commonplace elements. You have to ensure that there's a logic behind the process and that it isn't just a series of superimposed images that remain superficial and interchangeable. It must be a form of radical normality.   **Part of the special**

70

logic of village settlements is that they aren't constrained by the laws regarding the distance between buildings. This allows one to deal with proximity and distance differently; the narrow and the open alternate, interact. We're dense at the edges and generous in the center. The worst thing is when the buildings are all equally spaced; but when every plot is the same or when you have single-family houses on standard plots this is almost unavoidable. ... There are a couple of principles that one can learn from working with a village. First of all: Spaces and distances are defined by activities. A range of things should be possible. Production should be possible, as should play, privacy. Each of these activities requires different separating distances from different neighbors. This permits dense, borderless atmospheres. Density should certainly be a goal but this varies from place to place. Shaped by this approach the building forms in the village are heterogeneous, private, "irrational". Spaces that are open to a range of purposes are better than designated communal spaces. They promote freedom. Another aspect of space is that I should be able to retreat; see, but not be seen. ... And yet these are variations of rules that are determined by materials, processes, dimensions. The boundaries between public and private in the village are differentiated – there are clear boundaries and soft transitions. Here, green spaces are particularly important – we always begin with the free space. This must be generous and ensure orientation. This should be located in the

Rural density.

most valuable position – while the buildings occupy the less favored parts of the plot. This is how it always was in the village. Earlier, these areas were reserved for the harvest, now they're important free spaces, collective experiential spaces – for coming together, playing, working.

Workshop

**With our capacity for introspection and free will, we humans
are commonly regarded as the pinnacle of creation: our mastery
of our hands has liberated our minds. But when we consider
you growing up here we get another image. Here it's the feet
that come first. You were walking all day, always on your legs.
And more than just carrying you from here to there these also
perceive, balance, provide both support and stance.** The legs
measure not just space but also its character, they sense the
topography. The up and down, the slope of the field, the
breadth of the land, but also the movement around you, the
urgency or the tranquility of the herd. And after the legs come
the arms.

Hand and foot

**One could say that your life is repeating the evolutionary pro-
cess. By standing on two legs you free your arms and hands;
you follow your life as a farmer's lad by starting an apprenticeship with a carpenter. First walking, now handling. The hand,
coordinated by the eye, becomes the focus.** That's a good way
of putting it. Although anyone who can wield a sickle knows
how agricultural work is shaped by this interaction between the
legs, the arms, the hands, and the senses. But you're right: As
an aspiring craftsman I had to use my hands more carefully,
precisely, consciously. **Was this need for more care the dominant experience?** Possibly. One reaches, forms, moves, creates,

all with the hand. But one also touches something, feels it, senses it – one experiences reality much more directly than with the eye, the ear or the nose. Manual skills develop and these give time a new dimension. One reflects upon how one does something. Sensuality and reflection begin with the hands. ... I have the impression that a piece of work that was produced manually engages with me in a completely different way than one which was made otherwise. The hand remains in play. If an object is handmade I experience it differently. Is it possible to experience a building that's entirely based on geometrical ideas, that refers only to such logic, in the same way that one experiences a building that's been handed over, upon which hand has been laid? A building that reveals the act of being made, even when it's finished? In the first case it's as if I never truly engage with the building. I keep my distance, the object is abstract. ... In architecture this is certainly a problem. For what is the truth of architecture? According to Alexander Kluge, "concretion provides proof of the truth of good architecture." And this "reveals itself when the building is alive."[22]

Life is diversity. Our age knows only one God: reason. But it's more than questionable whether reason is so self-explanatory. Ernst Pöppel certainly noted that "everything is tightly related to everything else and these things influence each other in a quite unpredictable way,"[23] and "there's no such thing as an autonomous psychological condition."[24] The brain connects senses, emotions, memories, and intentional movements almost simultaneously. Abstractions leave some of these out – which, in

22 Kluge, Alexander: in Kramer, Ferdinand, Die Bauten, Wasmuth, Tübingen 2015, p. 98, transl. by R.H.
23 Pöppel, Ernst: Der Rahmen, dtv, Munich 2010, p. 113, transl. by R.H.
24 Pöppel, Ernst: Der Rahmen, dtv, Munich 2010, p. 113, transl. by R.H.

moderation, is also necessary. But something's always left behind. Where's the limit? Difficult to say. One shouldn't jump to conclusions! It's not as if all of these are always present to the same degree. There are strong places which are quite devoid of people – when I walk through our village and see everything that was made by hand I feel as if it's alive. The people are all around me, hidden in these things. Objects based completely on a rational abstract design can also succeed – so much is possible. But such objects are remote. ... Places whose surfaces only bear witness to mechanical production methods, where no one has laid a hand, can be quite alien. Laying a hand also means: leaving a trace, setting a sign. This brings the sign, the symbol, the cultural anchor into play – and here we mean the core of a symbol and not just its superficial image. If we use the image of the "nest" to em-body a sense of security – as we did in Disentis – we must express its essence successfully. A nest, this means density, proximity, warmth, it's a warm stone, timber, textile. Metaphors can show the path that leads to architecture of the highest quality. Working with metaphors in architecture is logical, but problem-

A nest of stone and warmth: Girls' Dormitory, Disentis, 2001–2004.

atic. One must avoid being trapped by an image, one must become spatial.

Handwork and machine

Things that aren't made by hand also say something about how they're produced. Industrial products are largely free of the human touch, remote-controlled. In some cases this is fine for

us, in others not. We can still tell the difference between a cheese from the dairy and one from the factory. And in the case of mass-produced objects such as cars, manual production is enjoying a renaissance in the luxury segment. There's a difference, and we can feel it. Aren't many of our desolate places explained by the fact that human input is only indirect? That machines and technology play the intermediary. Are there anthropological places which lack directness? The immediacy of manual production communicates itself through the object – a bodily experience becomes possible. The hand: the maker; the hand: the sensor – the two work together and make it possible to add something and receive something in return. But this isn't automatic. One must have learnt to deal with objects. Learning, practicing, using – each is somewhat different. And of course using something also always means asking: What for? **Did carpentry teach you that?** Strangely enough not at the beginning. At the beginning I focused on making – I wanted results. Feeling, perceiving, only came later – these need time, they only come with practice. **I'm initially interested in the concrete experience. An example from another trade: When I make dough my hands tell me when I have the temperature, the consistency, the texture, and the viscosity that'll ensure the success of my baking.**

Dough and wood

I know – from time to time I roll the dough with which my wife bakes our bread. So I also know how much it must be kneaded if it's going to succeed. This is felt by the hands, not seen by the eyes, smelt by the nose or heard by the ear. The hand is such an extraordinary sensory organ! **Is there any difference between this and – let's say – planing a wooden surface?**

Of course the touch of my hand tells me everything about the desired surface finish. What's more: Planing demonstrates that perception and doing are very closely related – how the plane is moving, what pressure is required, etc. But knowing what surface is right for the subsequent use is completely different. This requires expectation, intuition. It's the experience of the craftsman that has to deliver the answer: What am I making this for? What do I feel when I touch it, sit upon it, eat from it? What are the right dimensions, proportions?

Monotony and knowledge

Another experience related to your time as a craftsman: Quality emerges not from a rapid burst of cause and effect but as a result of long practice. Monotony is extremely important and fascinating. If you can put up with monotony you'll discover a lot. This leads to a vitality that's almost spatial. You can feel this very well in, for example, the Paternos Prayer for the Dead.[25] Repetition generates a wealth of spiritual experience – although the word experience seems too imprecise. Doing something repeatedly can become agonizing yet this is essential to learning a trade. Repetition shines brightest – is a wonderful phrase. If I want to change something, my experience is that I should do the same thing, over and over again. This allows me to see what's changing. **This is where the division into explicit and implicit knowledge comes into play. Explicit: This covers conscious, intentional actions. Implicit: These are the actions that have been translated into flesh and blood – kneading the dough, pedaling the bicycle, the knowledge of my hands, embedded knowledge. Taking this further: If a touch a**

---

25 Paternos: Roman Prayer for the Dead.

hot stove I pull my fingers away instantaneously before even my brain can react; the nerves have already interpreted the pain and triggered the necessary physical actions. Reflex and implicit knowledge work together. Implicit knowledge is principally the knowledge of that which is close by, explicit knowledge covers that which is further away. The skill of the craftsman is permeated by the transition between these forms of knowledge. So much so that back then even I had little awareness of the difference. We're completely convinced that everything occurs rationally. But one day in the workshop is enough to teach you that this isn't the case. There, a lot happens off the cuff – I grab a tool without looking; the plank out of which I should make a stool is in my hand long before I'm thinking about what I'm doing. It's hard to believe that so many people barely have an opportunity to experience this; they're probably doing other things, they're bankers, they're making plans. **Implicit knowledge establishes the framework that allows us to act explicitly.** The key thing is to be quite clear about this interrelationship, to learn something about it, to be able to employ it as a tool.

Beyond the plan

Which means, for example, that a building is more than that which is defined by the rational plan. Experiences, evaluations, memories, feelings – my own and those of others – are unavoidably present. This doesn't diminish the plan, but it puts it into perspective. Being clear about this can't just mean integrating these influences – where they're consciously available – into the plan, but that one should expect more. I experience this all the time: People who see something one way – and only one way. Yesterday I had such a conversation about windows.

I talked and talked, saying: But it opens in this direction and the wind hits the window and the building from here and the light doesn't shine in the reveal like it shines in the opening and the section has a role to play. But my interlocutor stuck to his line: No, a window is this and only this, just like it says in the dictionary. All other levels of experience remain excluded. Not a chance! Reason has defined it for him like that, clear, irrefutable. In contrast, knowledge based on experience, developed in the workshop is less clear cut because it's constantly renewing itself – a process that never ends.   **Aristotle might have been able to help him; he called the hand the first of all tools²⁶ – the extension of our self. Making things by hand and the manual experience gained in the process are autonomous activities. And they can make two things clear: Knowledge gained through practice is not the same as logical justification. And: The hand is capable of extraordinary things. We know today that the parts of the body and the sensory organs are governed by specific parts of the brain. And here we discover something astonishing: The hands occupy around a third of the volume of the brain dedicated to the entire human body. The volume of the brain dedicated to the hands is the same as the volume dedicated to the senses of seeing, hearing, and smelling. This is huge and underlines the hand's importance.**   That really is impressive! And it's dramatic for humanity if our hands no longer have anything

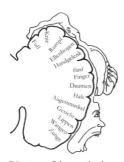

Diagram of the cerebral cortex showing discretionary human motor functions (from Penfield, Rasmussen). The enormous importance of the hand and vocal organs is clear.

---

26 Aristotle: "The hand is a tool of tools," in: De Anima IV 687 16–23.

to do. If the hand is neglected and manual skills are lost important areas of the brain will become unused and the brain as a whole will suffer. This lends a completely new dimension to manual labor. And this is particularly dramatic in an age in which we believe ourselves capable of rendering life completely transparent.

Improvisation

The versatility and interconnectedness of the hand become tangible in the versatility of handwork. The implicit knowledge learnt through practice provides the framework for explicit actions. Intuition is a cardinal virtue of the craftsman which can be employed in the form of improvisation. Before the design tool and the execution tool were combined – as is often the case today – handwork permitted this intermediate step. On the one hand there was a plan and, on the other hand, a more or less case-by-case combination of intuition, improvisation, and execution. Situational action. The question is: How can I employ this tool? I'm grateful that I was able to have this experience – to approach a solution via situational action. This is quite different from design as we generally understand it today: The plan has to cover everything. If I hadn't had this experience as a craftsman I wouldn't be aware of this situational link, of this "massive parallelism". **The electronic media are particularly responsible for creating the belief that the plan enables total mobilization and control, the belief that only things designed down to the last detail are worthy of our respect. Voices have been raised against this. Bruno Latour finds, for example, that: "There is no control and no all-powerful creator ... but there is care, scruple, cautiousness, attention, contemplation, hesitation and revival. To understand each**

other, all we have is what comes from our own hands, but that doesn't mean our hands can be taken as the origin."[27] Three things are meant by this: Interactions – which are characteristic of handwork – are preferable to one-dimensional processes. The work of the craftsman will stand the test. And finally: Having said all this, we're still not the (only) origin. Relationships certainly play a greater role in handwork. I never start at zero – there's the material, ability, practice – all of this is already there. And not everything is in my head – there are the senses, the hands, action and reaction. It's not just about: getting started, developing, finishing. There's also: considering, hesitating, compiling, looking back – all those things that seem to get in the way of today's processes. And I notice this in objects: Are they smooth, perfect, each one like the next? Or are they plastic, with small deviations and variations? The former are the work of machines, the latter of situational action. **Perfection, absolute control, and all-powerful creators who build something from nothing – that is self-empowerment which overestimates the role of the plan and the structure. Handwork, in contrast, is one element in a creative sequence, a metabolic form of the act of production. "The notion of making," insists Latour, "in no way entails that of an all-powerful maker."[28]** Indeed, we can all act as if we're part of a world that is a work in progress.[29] In architecture in particular this idea

---

27 Latour, Bruno: Rejoicing: Or the Torments of Religious Speech, transl. by Julie Rose, Polity Press, Cambridge 2013, p. 144.

28 Latour, Bruno: Rejoicing: Or the Torments of Religious Speech, transl. by Julie Rose, Polity Press, Cambridge 2013, p. 143.

29 Guzzoni, Ute: Der andere Heidegger, Verlag Karl Alber, Freiburg/Munich 2009, p. 108. "For Heidegger it's basically about – and with a radicalism that can't be radical enough – thinking about the essence of something ... as an occurrence, as movement ... This means that there is absolutely no danger of either hypostatization or essentialization." Transl. by R.H.

is hard to accept for those who want to create something that's never been done before – but this isn't important. More important is the question of how I can put a new spin on the world, reverse its polarities, chart a new course, choose a different option. I must participate, play along, and then it'll play along with me. ... They have big plans in the next valley; I find them monstrous. Let me put it like this: I can't simply go there and say: So, now I'm going to build a tower block in this valley. However, this doesn't mean: I'm only allowed to build old mountain huts. But rather: I should ensure that no shed is like any other; I should try to understand why this one is unlike that one and to be clear what I want to do otherwise and what I want to do the same. **Design differently?** Producing, creating – for one thing these are declining. It's not in our power to create an entire world. On the other hand, the process is becoming broader. There are so many contexts that have to be considered, that influence me, and that I can influence. Economics is one: a context of which we're always part; If we manage things well, we'll earn a bit, if we manage things badly, we'll be sawing away at the branch upon which we're sitting. But this isn't the same as that which we think of today as economics: that is business. Business is only interested in one aspect of the cake – how can I make my slice bigger at the expense of others?

Playing

Participate, get in tune, play along – you speak of situational links, experiencing "massive parallelism"[30] and learning to play with it ... If we could make this clearer with an example from another world? We always played football up here in summer – in the beginning we all played, young and old, on the dirt track, and later we boys had a pitch. I wanted to be a footballer. And when I stand on the pitch and receive the right pass I know without thinking that I must now score a goal. Did I reflect on this? I see the gap in the defense, my legs know where they have to run; an opponent wants to block my path so I pass automatically to a teammate, he runs upfield, returns the pass, my foot can read the angle and: Gooooal! That is "massive parallelism", presence, action – if thinking is useful at all then at best retrospectively. ... The thing about this is: You must let it happen. You have to be open to experiences – even bad ones. I must say yes, for good or ill. Some experiences hurt. As a designer I must expose myself to these and take the plunge. I learnt this as a craftsman, not that I was really aware of it at the time, that came later. I'd already gathered experience before: herding the animals, watching the meadows grow, the wind blow, the weather change – I was experiencing all that around me, unconsciously perhaps, but it was all there and maybe this world has remained more important to me than the workshop. **That's all so real in comparison with our lives today. The man / machine debate has also applied to the communications industry for half a century. Machines organize**

---

30 "Every state of awareness is marked by a spatiotemporal pattern of neuronal activities in which several regions participate; the activity of just one area, the 'center,' isn't enough." Ernst Pöppel: Der Rahmen, dtv, Munich 2010, p. 428. See also note 23, transl. by R.H.

repetitive actions according to a principle and the communications machine originally did this too, structuring data processing and saving data – in contrast with humans with their body and spirit, hand and brain. Now there's a new aspect: thanks to feedback loops the machine is becoming autonomous – keyword artificial intelligence. The merger of man and machine should soon be complete. The question of where this will lead depends not least upon whether this question was posed in 2000 or 2017 – will the machine become as intelligent as man or will man become as dumb as the machine? The Israeli historian Y. N. Harari describes how efficiency and control are permeating our lives. He expects life expectancy to increase due to our growing concern about our health. Control and protection will intensify. Our expectations in general and our demand for flexibility and resilience in particular will rise. Support systems, from technical equipment to psychoactive substances, will become ubiquitous and we will ask who can afford all this. Skeptical voices can already be heard today: "Our life is much more comfortable than that of previous generations yet I doubt that we are happier than people were a century ago. ... It's quite obvious that technical possibilities can't simply be translated into happiness."[31] Can we bear all this innovation? Man wants to be autonomous, to run his own life, which is why he'll only put up with these machines up to a certain point. Machines can be very valuable if I know what I want – see the Internet. But if you don't exercise your own will they'll overrun you.

---

31 Harari, Yuval Noah: Die Welt wird extrem hektisch sein, in: SZ Magazin 38, 22.09.2017, p. 41, transl. by R.H.

Autonomy

This shows me that autonomy is becoming important, however relative this may be. Standing on your own two feet: Such "personality development" is well served by taking a concrete, careful approach to things, by doing them yourself – you learn this as a craftsman, through the interactions and improvisations of your trade. How well do I deal with the things that happen to me? Chance is the great enemy of the machine. The machine might become intelligent but will it become wise? And what about moods, feelings? The development of these is part of personality. **Autonomy is a good cue. Thanks to the Internet we're increasingly seeing not only concrete statements but also speculation, insinuation, and allegation reaching a new, higher level. The way that a very thorough, scientifically tested study about insect population levels[32] could so rapidly become caught up in a whirlwind of conspiracy theories and quasi-religious debate driven by special interests and hostility is – to use a new word for once – crass! The possibility of debating the issue on a subjective level is lost – irrevocably?[33]** We're distancing ourselves from our surroundings, losing our sense of our own body. Just like in building where we immediately turn to the latest technology when, for example, the issue is energy. We're disappearing as a user, forfeiting our autonomy. **So who's controlling whom, playing with whom?** Digitalization will change our approach to the mountains. But whether the digital workplace is a positive thing? ... It could turn out differently. The Internet tells a tourist that the sun's shining in Vrin; he sets off in his car; but when he's here the weather turns and

---

32 Study of the death of insects carried out by the Entomologischer Verein Krefeld e.V.
33 Grossarth, Jan: Insektensterben als Medienhysterie?, in: FAZ 14.2.17, p. 15.

the modern guest leaves. He who seeks to control the world in such a way is not a reliable guest. The image has replaced the reality. ... Years ago there was a project in Surselva which tried to encourage people to stay with the help of digital media. No one was encouraged to stay; emigration actually accelerated. However, the inn in Valendas and several other tangible projects in the village did attract visitors. Digitalization has global dimensions and doesn't address the characteristics of the periphery. And its real benefits for mountain regions are also likely to be modest. I don't see the digital world as a threat – but as a promise? Does it really touch us so deeply? **Do we have to go as far as Steven Hill, who speaks of a "techno-Potemkin village"?**[34]   Who knows? What I do know is that – as Heidegger once said – the tangibility and the solidity of handwork are real. Such a message gets around. It's not a question of proclaiming a new elixir but of simply recognizing what we already have – what has already proved itself – and then of putting this in a new perspective and insisting that it's as valid as the latest machine and that the entire salvation of the world isn't dependent upon the next innovation. "Still we can act otherwise," says Heidegger in his Messkirch lecture. "We can confirm the unavoidable use of technical devices and also deny them the right to dominate us and so to warp, confuse, and lay waste our nature."[35]

34 Hill, Steven: Die Start-up Illusion, Knaur, Munich 2017, p. 135, transl. by R.H.
35 Heidegger, Martin: Discourse on Thinking, transl. by John M. Anderson and Hans Freund, Harper & Row, New York, Evanston and London 1966, p. 54.

The whole

The hand remains central. The anthropologist Andre Leroi-Gour-han draws attention to the close relationship between the hand and the mouth.[36] An unborn child "practices" eating using its thumb while still in the womb – a relationship that stays with us. The mouth more or less formulates clear sounds as a means of communicating with others, sounds and gestures, mouth and hand complement each other, initially as equals. Eventually it's the hand that supports speech over the long term: through writing. The hand and the mouth ensure that man remains a social being. Speaking, doing, these are always social. One is part of society – one cannot withdraw from it. Hence, I can ask:

What can I achieve as part of society? Should I improve it? Does this not apply particularly to architecture, the most social of all arts? But even an architecture that fails to do this can't escape from this relationship. It only turns its back on the question. Even aesthetic questions have a social dimension – and vice-

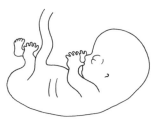

An interaction from the very start: hand and mouth – feeding, gestures, speech, writing.

versa. Today we can name the powers that are seeking to turn their back on society, to shirk their social responsibility. What's the significance of the fact that these are exactly the same powers whose signature buildings display such an enormous aesthetic appetite? What does this say about this aesthetic? ... The reality remains that we are social beings and part of society.

---

36 Leroi-Gourhan, André: Gesture and Speech, transl. by Anna Bostock Berger, MIT Press, Cambridge, Massachusetts 1993. André Leroi-Gourhan, 1911–86, French archaeologist, paleontologist, and anthropologist. Professor at the Sorbonne and the Collège de France. Focused on technology and the culture of materials.

I can influence, improve things when I accept this, admit to this reality, and take the context into account. Context isn't just my built surroundings but also the social, historical, and psychological aspects of the space in which I act. This could also be a place of "massive parallelism". I can have an impact when I allow myself to get involved. In this case my body would be the counterpart of the context – although I'm not only referring here to my mere physical body but also to the space in which I operate. Architecture emerges if this interaction addresses the whole, if the built objects reflect this. I'm interested in places,

Bridge, Heidelberg.

good places, and these are more than a mere thing, an isolated, free-standing object. A built object reflects the relationships that prevail in a place and must, naturally, be of high quality. But which sort of quality? Is geometry alone enough? Good, strong objects have the ability to shape a space. In his book "Building Dwelling Thinking" Heidegger chose the example of a bridge.[37]

Place

This object, "the bridge," gives rise to the place. It connects the riverbanks, brings together the paths, the landscape, the people. Thing and place are closely interrelated. This is rarely the case with today's architectural "objects". These are dominated by distance, the desire to stand out, to attract attention. The object stands for itself, sets itself apart, avoids relationships.

37 Heidegger, Martin: Building Dwelling Thinking, in: Poetry, Language, Thought, transl. by Albert Hofstadter, Harper Colophon, New York, 1971, p. 152.

Relationships are important but not one-sided. A strong object imposes itself on a weak context, creates relationships. But then the object responds to the context by awakening dormant potential. Just as it's hard to imagine such objects without a context, it's also hard for objects to create a context of their own. It's the interaction that matters. **Heidegger notes: The place isn't a sort of empty receptacle which is already there before the objects are created. It's the bridge that transforms the location on the river into a place. But it has to be a suitable location, one that permits a bridge to be built.** And the importance of these objects varies, hierarchies play a role: That's how it is in the village. Some built objects are more significant and some less – the village church, the ordinary buildings. There are signs that enable us to orient ourselves within the social system. People search for orientation – and "strong" objects help. Christian Norberg-Schulz insisted upon this close relationship between people and places: **"Human identity presupposes the identity of place."[38] "Strong" objects, such as buildings, deploy their impact when they're able to resonate.** The object can resonate when it interacts with society. When it finds itself surrounded by social activity it can trigger events. Resonance can occur when built structures and people come together. This is the basis for resonance to happen. … In Valendas I saw the innkeeper crossing the square where he met the kitchen hand who was carrying a basket of strawberries – did that happen or did I just imagine it? This image created a space in which life happens.

38 Norberg-Schulz, Christian: Genius Loci, Academy editions, London 1980, p. 22.

Up the mountain

If I want to influence, I must be open to influence ...   ... and can't predetermine it. Everything that congregates there comes from one's own experiential space. It can't be defined. Everything that one perceives, feels, takes, remembers, even moves and does, merges together, creates a critical mass that can't be divided up. When this critical mass has been reached it becomes an interesting tool. Is this the answer to my question: Where do ideas come from? What are these "meltdowns"? The older I become, the more easily they happen. Earlier it was a lot harder – how I suffered! I tried to summon up an idea but nothing happened. And then suddenly something's there – I can't explain. The fact that this is easier today may have something to do with practice, composure, openness, and the simple certainty that something will happen. Although my expectations have risen I don't struggle like I used to. Continuous doing, perseverance, practice helps – I learnt this from my experience of handwork and my childhood as a farmer's lad. **It sounds as if the anthropologist André Leroi-Gourhan visited you fifty years ago on the Maiensäss and, upon returning to the modern world, asked: "Freed from tools, gestures, muscles, from programming actions, from memory, freed from the imagination by the perfection of the broadcasting media, freed from the animal world, the plant world, from cold, from microbes, from the unknown world of mountains and seas, zoological Homo sapiens is probably nearing the end of his career. ... How shall this archaic mammal, with its archaic needs that have been the driving force of its ascent, continue to push its rock up the hillside if one day it is left with only the image of its**

reality?"[39] He was able to ask this because he knew both worlds. If we want to retain this same ability we must be careful to relinquish neither.

Composure
Physical and mechanical, situational and sequential, place and object — a wide arc. After intensive investigation the anthropologist André Leroi-Gourhan concluded that handwork is the form of culture in which art, the social aesthetic, and the appreciation of technology have become most individual.[40] **How do you experience the world of today?** The fragmentation of the whole, the optimization of the fragment, and the culture of the specialist dominate the scene today. This is a world of professionals, "who provide solutions". Every element must fit and work from the very start. Whether it all works 'as a whole' doesn't bother them. Architectural quality isn't created, things get done. But I don't just want to get things done. ... Take the Mortuary for example: Many people wanted the burials to be carried out quickly. I wanted to create enough room for the ritual of laying out, for the unhurried farewell, to allow the final journey in a small procession to take place with dignity. I insisted upon this. Upon laying the path. And then people understood. **Getting things done, this fascinates people today. It shapes today's design process. Nothing should remain open, everything must be resolved before building work can start. This is far from being the only way to build, as anyone who started building fifty years ago or who has experience of**

39 Leroi-Gourhan, André: Gesture and Speech, transl. by Anna Bostock Berger, MIT Press, Cambridge, Massachusetts 1993, p. 407.

40 Leroi-Gourhan, André: Gesture and Speech, transl. by Anna Bostock Berger, MIT Press, Cambridge, Massachusetts 1993.

other parts of the world still knows – he understands the hand-work culture.   There was an interaction between a range of scales, not everything was defined right down to the last detail from the very start, the participants coordinated their work, had to take account of everyone's ability – that's how such quality was produced. One didn't merely do one's bit and disappear. What matters today? The finished plan, the checklist, boxes are ticked, minutes written, the controller is in charge. That's how the professionals do it. Every man for himself without taking any notice of his neighbor, minimal responsibility. In theory this is optimal but, in practice, it's questionable – as we can see all around us. As an approach it hardly does justice to architecture – in which the whole is more than the sum of its parts. ... Of course such quality requires a counterpart, someone who knows what it is. Quality isn't simply there. Of course we have to get things done but we also have to evaluate what's important. What do we want? What should this become? What's required in order to achieve it? It's no help at all if a building is beautifully detailed but doesn't touch our hearts, doesn't resonate. Just knowing exactly what the focus should be requires time for concentration, composure, intuition. That's how architecture is created. And even if this density only arises for a moment – then I'm still happy.

A table

You've recently returned to being a carpenter, a furniture maker. What's behind this?   A house is a house, a hearth is a hearth. Our memories store characteristic images of houses, hearths, tables. These are shaped by culture and help me to organize my thoughts or, in other words: to design. One thing I particularly like in Vrin is the clear hierarchy of church, school, house, barn, garden. ... I can work well with this hierarchy. It's this relationship that explains the significance of the buildings of the village. **And yet each is unique. Let's take this house in the village that you designed around fifteen years ago. It has a typical façade, plastic, strongly expressive, and details such as the exposed battens to the stone cladding which form a sort of cornice. It clearly wasn't enough for you to create a house as a simple box. It's unique yet it fits in with the neighbors.**

The new buildings don't need to be artworks compared with the old ones but they should be artfully built – with care and commitment. There are many ways of doing this; by playing with individual elements like these battens. That's the trick. And that's also what interests me

Barn, Vrin.

about furniture. Finding something commonplace that has symbolic energy; unearthing something that's anchored deep in the memory. Something with which you can play, create something artistic. Caminada the carpenter was still quite unaware of all this ...

Commonplace

This revived interest in furniture is due to the commission by a Swiss furniture manufacturer to develop furniture "from the mountains." Can I put it like that? Perhaps: They want to replace shiny surfaces with objects that mean something – you could say: with other values, or: with values *per se*. How do we

93

do this? Of course a weird creation, a wondrous object, can also lay claim to having values. But I'm more interested in finding values in feelings that we share deep down, in bringing these to the surface, experiencing them. In this sense values have something to do with place, with belonging: They can be located, allocated. **They can be located. Does this mean that they're a common feature in a place?** I'd assume so. That they're common. And if I then play with them a little they become uncommon and, hence, alive. It's a subtle game, not the grand gesture. ... So: rather than seeing a table as an interesting technoid structure or exciting sculpture I ask: What is a table? First of all it consists of three elements: top, frame, leg. I learnt this in the workshop. I have to understand these elements, alone, in relation to each other, in relation to other

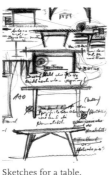

things. Then: Do these elements have a hierarchy? Which is the most important? – the tabletop. The leg is also important, but in another way; and, in yet another way: the frame. I start with the tabletop – can I create a relationship with the user, communicate values? The origin of the material, the meaning of symbols or the relationship with the table maker can create such values.

Sketches for a table.

Belonging, normality: What triggers these? I circle around this question. **These circles lead to something other than a horizontal surface, vertical supports, and right angles. That would be the normal solution of our culture, but your commonplace has something extra**. An extra nudge that sets the commonplace vibrating. In the handwork culture every commonplace element is individually worked, varied – it's as far removed from a dull copy as it is from a tasteful creation.

A thing lives because it's been worked on by somebody in a place rich in references – as Heidegger puts it: The thing things.[41] **How can this be understood in terms of the design process?** I firstly dissected, dismantled, and examined the individual elements in an attempt to understand them. How autonomous are they, how strong is the relationship between them? At the same time I search for their meaning, personally, as a human, as a living being. I discover: Each element has a certain autonomy – only in this way are relationships possible. If one combines these energies, the unexpected can happen. **In the case of the table, what happened concretely?** Well, the legs became tapered although they still have a square section. They perform different functions, are more technical elements. And besides: They spread outwards – more or less imperceptibly. This is important to me. It shouldn't be too obvious because otherwise it loses all its mystery. This is how tension, action is created. This action doesn't take place, it's only hinted at. For me this is almost erotic: Is something going to happen here or is it just my imagination? An interaction that remains exciting. A further aspect: Type and topos are also relevant for a table. The legs can follow a general typology, one that's proven itself; but the tabletop can be individualized, by local materials or human preference. But despite such variations the table should still belong to the table family. **Here's a picture of the table. And here are the special elements. I touch the table on the tabletop, that's where the relationship is most physical.** In the case of the chair this is the back; and, in a slightly different

---

41 Heidegger, Martin: Bremen and Freiburg Lectures: Insight Into That Which Is and Basic Principles of Thinking, trans. By Andrew J. Mitchell, Indiana University Press, Bloomington 2012, p. 12.

way, the seat. These areas are designed traditionally. One is very close to me, the other less so. I want to celebrate this in different ways.

Material, space

The result is a hierarchy of values. Does the same apply to materials?   This depends upon what something's being used for. The things that I touch should feel good, flatter me. Not every material is suitable for this. Regarding glass tabletops, for example, my physical experience says: nonsense. ... At the moment we're asking a little too much of, trusting a little too much in materials as such. Sometimes this is a real challenge. But I'm interested in something else. How do I create meaning? How we use things, how we live, it's important to me that we take these questions seriously. It's important to encounter things calmly, to let them come to me, to remain open-minded. Whether I'm dealing with furniture or buildings: Only in this way will we create what Heidegger called a new down-to-earthness.[42] What form can this have?   **Relationships have an impact here. Something suggests something else, a context emerges.** If I establish a relationship with my context, meaning is created, I'm rooted. This makes sense, something of value can emerge and take form.   **These issues are beyond calculation. Your buildings sometimes have elements that make a mockery of calculation. Such as the internal columns of the forest hut or the external ones of the sawmill in Cons. Those are definitely massive. What's that about?**   About space. That's what architecture's about. If the cross section of the columns in the For-

42 Heidegger, Martin: Discourse on Thinking, transl. by John M. Anderson and Hans Freund, Harper & Row, New York, Evanston and London 1966, p. 53.

est Hut is greater than structurally necessary then the space has a different quality. The structural optimum wouldn't have produced the effect that I wanted: to contrast the opening of the space onto the uncertainty of the forest with the certainty of this solidity. **Space not as a characterless Cartesian expanse but as the opposite: something defined by quality.** Cer-

Forest Hut, Domat/ Ems, 2013.

tainly. A twofold relationship: contrast, but also unity: both in wood. The alien returns home, outside becomes inside, the warmth of wood is used knowingly. ... Today, the cost of material plays a minor role compared with the cost of labor. This was an issue at the sawmill in Cons. We had wood from the forest, tall trunks that were far too thick. And we had the three brothers from the sawmill who could wield a chainsaw better than certain people can wield a knife and fork. So they took their tools and joined the trunks, built a house with logs and chainsaws, turned ability into architecture. **Excess material balanced by the mastery of the chainsaw and outdoing every modern high-tech timber building with its calculated joints.** A wonderful idea and a wonderful structure. But here it's also about meaning and this is defined by: what, when, how. This amazing work with the chainsaw isn't ideal everywhere. What the three sawyers built outside the village wouldn't be appropriate at its heart.

Minimal intervention

And yet: the fascination of this direct, raw intervention remains — not least as a proposition in view of the growing trend towards refinement. That can be countered: Handwork is always refinement. Although: It depends how it's done. It's usually focused. And it's not an end in itself. The craftsman is sparing in his use of refinement and finishing. If everything's perfect, the effect is lost. I can remember my mother telling me that when my grandfather returned from one of his trips across the Greina, he brought back something small that made the whole house glow. ... If we look around this part of Vrin we can see all sorts of material: lots of wood, but also semi-finished industrial products, the carefully built alongside the abandoned, the valuable alongside the banal. If it's well-built this Eternit wall can certainly hold its own alongside wooden shingles or boarding. Isn't the decisive question how it's done, how it's used? An object wrapped in plastic can add a dash of blue. And the satellite dish: Just forget the junk, in a few years technology will have replaced it. **Is that a diagnosis or a prognosis? We can see that the world of objects, of manufactured industrial products, is driving out the things developed through use. Our food has finally become industrialized. The number of consumer articles is multiplying rapidly: By what factor does the number of apps grow every day? And at the same time we hear a growing lament over our loss of control and our surrender to the inevitable. Is any reversal of this trend in sight?** Of course it's like this. But, on the other hand: Precisely because it's like this it won't stay like this. I'm astonished by the conservatism of trend researchers and cultural prophets as they make their predictions about the future. The life of the farmer up here has certainly changed – driven by technology. But how will technology develop next? Are other, even several, directions conceivable? In our valley the farmers produce food with the help of technology but this food is definitely not industrially optimized. And this has enabled them to establish a secure market position.

Cultural hegemony

This suggests that it's not about technology itself but about the question of 'how'; This is a question for producers, consumers — a question of culture. Gramsci said: It's not about technology but cultural hegemony.[43] **It's to do with winning minds. That's what you've been fighting for.**   We want to establish a school for craftspeople in Graubünden because we're convinced that, alongside agriculture and tourism, handwork represents an opportunity for the countryside. I think that they're interrelated. Handwork can attract tourists. But I'm talking about real interdependency – not the usual tourist marketing strategy which, in reality, is a cultural sellout. The production of organic meat is flourishing up here. And just like agriculture, handwork is also no longer part of the subsistence economy. The countryside can be a manufacturing location, can liaise with the production in the towns. Let me return to our project "Furniture from the Mountains": Serial elements like the table legs can come from the town (type), and the tabletops from special workshops across the region (topos) – sometimes from Valais, sometimes from Graubünden. ... This school is a joint initiative with Austria and Northern Italy. The aim is to deepen knowledge about the handwork tradition. If we speak about high-quality products with a local connection then this must be much more tangible. Today's handwork must know more about culture, its own culture. Craftspeople must also be better at selling themselves; elsewhere this is known as corporate culture. And of course they must also be open to new materials and techniques. Crossover can inspire.   **Handwork is a cultural resource which could be lost, has already partly been lost. The**

43 Gramsci, Antonio: Philosophie der Praxis, Frankfurt 1967, p. 416.

old buildings up here were sparingly decorated through the restrained use of wooden carving. Yet they feel so assured compared with much that today's architecture is trying to recreate. This is another sign of change, like the change in our choice of food, in our eating habits. Hardly anyone would dare to serve a Toast Hawaii at a party anymore. There are some notable initiatives in this area, such as the development of an Alpine cuisine – although there's a clear risk of this becoming an elite cuisine. **Do we have to be so afraid of the elite? Aren't initiatives always started by small numbers of people?** It's a balancing act. Industry brought us many great things. But then they had to smarten these up using design. This wasn't enough, this design proliferated. And the latest trend is the commercialization of the innate, the everyday – the regional. This remains superficial; it requires feedback. This is a process of approximation. Then we can marvel and ask: Isn't the innate really good? And then we must keep on working, on the ornament, for example, that I mentioned before. Without understanding it will be hollow, as transient as rotten timber. **The extent to which the handwork culture can be on the cutting edge is demonstrated by a figure like Frank Lloyd Wright. This revolutionary of the art of building developed forms of expression that shaped American architecture throughout the 20th century. These began in the handwork tradition and now belong to the basic vocabulary of the modern movement. This could happen because the cultural environ-**

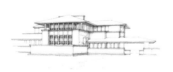

Frank Lloyd Wright, Willits House, 1902.

ment was conducive to this approach. Who says that this is unique? Today's environment is different but the interconnections could be related; we've forgotten how to ask such questions. This is what we must debate. We're seeking to make a "normal" table – normal for here. Because elsewhere it would be different. This means that we have to sharpen our perception – including in the area of aesthetics.

Good places

Those were aspects of your dream of creating a school. But why here? Something like this must occur in a specific place. If such things are developed in urban centers they touch no one. But if this happened in Vrin or at Disentis or Müstair Abbey the effect would be completely different. We wanted to convince local or regional companies but had very little success. The freaks from the cities are easy to convince. **Technical innovation is an issue. Industry, together with the trade associations and schools, fob off the craftspeople: But we make everything so well and so cheaply, you only have to build it in – but, please, as quickly and efficiently as possible, as rationally as a machine, a production line or a robot. Such technology isn't compatible with craftspeople. Steven Hill, an author from Silicon Valley, warns us Europeans against wanting to become a "clone of the USA" in the area of digitalization. It's much more important to find solutions for medium-sized businesses than for major companies. "My urgent advice to young digital entrepreneurs and prospective start-up hipsters: Leave Berlin, get out of Munich and Hamburg. Go to Meschede."[44] Should one add: Get out of Zurich, go to – why not – Vrin?** The context is certainly complex. It's not only about production but also about materials. Someone who works with industrialized timber products doesn't have to know how wood behaves, this is already a

---

44 Hill, Steven: Die Start-up Illusion, Knaur, Munich 2017, p. 160, transl. by R.H.

process of alienation. In contrast, the most interesting crafts-people are those who say: That doesn't interest me. They're only interested in knowing: What is my basic material and what is it capable of? But the allure of industry is very tempting. **In Germany there are hints of a change; fewer and fewer people want to eat half chickens from the poultry factory. Perhaps you're even more advanced and this isn't an issue any more?** In actual fact we've had a lot of success in recent years in the region in developing organic brands, and also in defining places like Vrin in terms of knitted construction. This won't necessarily continue. It would be the role of such a school to address this. Self-reflection – by a place, by a trade. In the olden days culture emerged, as it were, more easily, almost spontaneously, but today we have to reflect, evaluate, decide. Technical know-how isn't enough – this is about our place in the world and finding this requires energy. **Alone, one is quickly overstretched. One needs allies, especially allies from the city.**

Knitted construction

After your apprenticeship and some time working as a carpenter you made the big step: out into the valley, out into the world. Zurich School of Applied Arts, art school in Florence, and then back to Zurich for post-diploma studies at the ETH. The path towards building was clear. At the same time you were always taking the path back to Vrin and you began to build: here, building on the existing. And you spent years engaged in a striking examination of the vernacular way of building up here: knitted construction.

Type

This is a way of using wood that's fundamentally different from the post and beam structures or timber frames of the lower valleys. Rather than erecting posts and connecting these with beams, trunks are laid upon trunks and interlocked — knitted together — at the corners. Alvin Seifert speaks of timber masonry. One finds knitted construction throughout the Alps, but also along the arc of the Carpathians and up to Scandinavia. After all, laying trunks upon each other is far easier than fixing them upright, connecting them, and securing them using pins, joints, and struts. But "knitting" also produces its own logic – constructional, geometrical, and spatial. **The similarity of the**

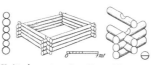

Knitted construction. From: Hermann Phleps: Holzbaukunst, der Blockbau, Karlsruhe 1942.

timber cross-sections and the lengths required to produce a uniform wall tends towards a square. But it's never a precisely measured, exact square. Up here it's generally a slightly elongated rectangle. It's the use of the space that's paramount, the geometry is secondary. Which is not to say: It isn't there. But the avoidance of pure shapes also reflects a sense of restraint; deviation creates tension. It's good when you can't see the intention. If one's negligent one tolerates the perfect. But perfection can become intolerable – for it allows no deviation. The buildings here in the valley were built like this, in the next valley like that, distinguishable yet very similar. This demonstrates the power of continuing to build in an almost identical way. **And for you at this time this means knitted construction, which is typical up here and enjoys a long tradition.** For me it's tradition and type that have stood the test. It's this belief that enables me to take knitting further. And it means that as I build I repeat, correct, proceed in a practiced manner, all of which is more or less a synonym for quality. Here in Vrin livelihoods were modest, there was a limited number of options, in both materials and technology. This led almost inevitably to this building type, which one was always seeking to improve – in relatively small steps. At first it was just about improving a tough existence. Then one explored other possibilities – but as far as I remember the space was restricted, one couldn't see the room for maneuver. When you're fighting for survival on the mountain you turn to the most obvious solution. But at certain moments there was this game, this curiosity for something new, something different – which is important because it allows you to see what you already have. This, however, requires space and that was very limited. Today we have a lot more space and we must learn to handle it properly – to play this game with variations in such a way that the meaning, the valuable, isn't lost. **At first glance the image of the buildings up here is one of great homogeneity – but at second glance none is like any other. There are different constructional solutions, and there's also enough decoration – which appears like an accessory added to the useful. Couldn't it possibly be the other way round: Isn't it this game, this trying out, that inspires improvement?** The type is paramount, this remains recognizable. The buildings are alike, but finely nuanced, which reveals a sophisticated spirit, and the desire to shed this straitjacket. Yet the buildings are very similar – and this question of 'almost identical' wouldn't let me go, became a quality. Identical simply means: congruent, an exact copy. That would be monotony, that would be bad. The 'almost identical', on the other hand, fascinates, shapes a place, has a powerful effect. This creates identity. And there's no identity without difference. This is why difference is so important in my architecture. Differences can't be allowed to disappear, without differences there's no identifiable belonging. It's like a game.

The game
Indeed, Ludwig Wittgenstein made the game one of the main subjects of his late observations. He speaks of the language game and of the fact that this underpins the meaning of an element in use. "The meaning of a word is its use in the language."[45] Analogously one could say: Things gain meaning through being used. This is a serious game. Things change,

---

45 Wittgenstein, Ludwig: Philosophical Investigations, transl. by G.E.M.Anscombe, Macmillan, New York 1953, p. 21.

gain a distinctive character. This can apply to the front door, but also to the wall cladding, a canopy. This happens in the context of a type that has stood the test, because we can deal with it.   **In Wittgenstein's concept this game of games, the use of words, establishes rules whose legitimacy is based on nothing other than the fact that they're valid. Use lends legitimacy, but use isn't a higher truth that exists in isolation.**   Type developed through use, this is how a place found its own rules. The game, on the other hand, is to do with escaping. Life is about breaking rules, but rules are set by life – this is an interaction. Breaking free from such limitations was also always an objective. And yet: Take care, don't break the rules of the game, because this only brings suffering.   **The game of football comes to mind – you were an enthusiastic player. A game without rules is unimaginable. Incidentally, one of the few new rules of the last seventy years was the decision in 1950 that FIFA games should be played wearing shoes. Does that make the game "more real"? The rules of a game become real when the game is played. Only then do they have any meaning. Conversely: The game can only flourish freely because it has rules. And what are rules when the players aren't free?**   Football shows how something can become effective. Sepp Herberger once said that if you want to enjoy something you must take it seriously.[46] And yet the player must be relaxed. Intensively relaxed? The same rules apply worldwide but the Brazilians and Germans have different approaches. The Brazilians dance with the ball glued to their feet while the Germans have this unbelievable drive, and when one of them isn't up to scratch

---

46 Herberger, Sepp: quoted by Michael Langer: Fußball, sein Leben, broadcast to mark his 70th birthday, Deutschlandfunk, 10.10.2006.

he'll be substituted. You can't do this in architecture. **The intense work with knitted construction in your architecture is almost a game.**

The first steps

Yes, and at the beginning I adopted everything quite uncritically. One needs time before one really starts to think. Initially I stuck rigidly to the rules, I wanted to play, I didn't want to be substituted. I didn't want to get a red card; after all, I kept getting yellow ones. Without trust you've very little chance. **Then the new ideas come. As far as I can see you started by building barns where you knitted using a system of elements.**

It was knitting, but without the massiveness of knitted construction. Every year I was commissioned to design a barn – big buildings, even if they weren't as big as they are today, quickly, using standardization. So we developed prefabricated timber-framed elements which we "knitted" together. I was interested in recognizability. It was important to me to be able to pass such a barn and see something 'almost identical'; it reminds me that I'm in a special cultural setting.

Barns 1996–2004.
Knitting with frame components.

The key elements are no longer the superimposed logs but the corners and the connections between the wall panels. Most of the wall of the barn is clad with planks and the knitted elements can only be seen in a few places. So these must be strong. Such toying with the observer awakes their interest. They can see enough to know what's going on. Not naked, but decently covered. Arousing. **Then there are buildings where we see the logs again but they're spaced apart**

rather than tightly joined – the wall becomes a breezy structure. Like the barns at the Abattoir.   These contain a hay-drying machine and I wanted to retain the option of returning to

drying using fresh air. The log structure is stable. It's a means of expressing my suspicion that the way we deal with hay today has no long-term future. I wanted to keep other paths open, not define every last detail. Could this be the source of

Abattoir, Vrin, 1998. Knitted surface.

my idea of the purpose-free? This has become increasingly important. Offering possibilities without insisting upon them, forcing them, keeping options open ... this creates ambiguity which is essential to me. And this requires something strong, standalone, autonomous. Part of the architectural debate embodied by the 2016 Biennale – which demands more society and participation on the one hand and purely autonomous architecture on the other – appears to me to come up short. I want more social engagement on the part of an architecture that is autonomous; authoritative but not exclusive. Not diagrammatic but continuously challenged by society, place, topos. At the end of the day a good building must say: I'm not a thing, an object, I'm somebody, a partner for you. It must contain ambiguity, openness. This leads to mutual relationships.

Maturity
Some years later you find yourself very close again to the original rules of knitted construction: log upon log, knitted corners. Now the focus is on the structure, the fact that the wall can support itself because it's vertically integrated. Almost inevita-

bly it becomes three-dimensional, the wall as body.   And now it's become a beautiful game. Applying the rules to find out how far one can go and then stop before it all comes crashing down. The basic principle is the cell – this holds everything together. The corners are distinctive but these have to be closed to become a continuous frame at which point the structure will stand. This opens up the entire range of possibilities and we can design freely before we reach the limits of this way of building which are determined by the length of the wall openings.   **One has the impression that maturity has been reached, as have certain standards in terms of, for example, dimensions. Most of these solid timbers have a cross section of 12 cm/20 cm.**   Yes, today we think that we know what the limit is. And I'm convinced that we can't go beyond this. If you want to do so you must forget knitted construction and look for another system. Knitting is good but beyond these dimensions – stop! One has to understand the logic behind the construction, then one recognizes its limits; then limits make sense. We tested this system on numerous houses and continuously achieved new results in terms of dimension and atmosphere. The range is broad and it's becoming broader as I try new combinations – knitted construction with wooden panels or shingle, a masonry core with a knitted shell, as in Haus Rumein, or even a knitted core with a masonry shell, as in Fürstenbruck. Knitted construction has, incidentally, been clad for

Haus Walpen, 2002.

Haus Segmüller, 2001.

a long time but we've only been celebrating this aesthetically for a generation.

Ritual

The notion of the spatial cell as the core of knitted construction refers not only to the space itself but also to the walls that define that space. The Mortuary is a prime example of this, the knitting has almost become a ritual – use and construction correlate to a high degree. Addressing death may not be an everyday architectural task but according to Loos[47] this is exactly where it begins. For me, the Mortuary was one of the most intense architectural challenges that I've faced. More precisely: It wasn't death but the denial of death that was the issue. The struggles with the village about the spaces dedicated to leave-taking, commemoration, transition. Ritual is a decisive help in dealing with grief, the main issue at "Stiva da morts", – it guarantees continuity and uniqueness. There has to be a careful balance between preservation and transformation ... paths play a decisive role. The building has two entrances, the visitor decides which to use. It has two rooms, one for the laying-out, one for collective or individual reflection. It has just one exit: The coffin is carried to the cemetery via the streets and the square of the village. **The emphasis on the joints in knitted construction seems to make it ideal for this building.** The issues are connection and transition. The knitted connection between the logs is revealed at the decisive interface between the two rooms, at this point one understands the construction of the walls: the double skin becomes a closed cell. The windows are narrow and have different

---

47 Loos, Adolf: Ornament and Crime, in: Trotzdem, Vienna 1982 (Innsbruck 1931), p. 78.

depths, creating alternating niches. The window becomes a space in itself, you can decide what you want to see or if you want to be seen at all. ... The transition is marked by a special timber threshold over which the coffin is carried. The building itself combines profane and sacred space, adding a new element to the hierarchy of building types in the village. ... The treatment of the wood differentiates the building from normal knitted construction: Painted on the outside with white casein it seeks to connect with the church, whose whitewashed stone walls have been refined in a similar way. In the interior the timber is also refined: with shellac. The wood has a special luster.

Stairwell in "Stiva da morts". Knitting, in four directions, becomes a spatial cell.

Theme and variation

The interior of the building almost has the character of a musical instrument. This suggests parallels between the development potential of this constructional approach and the idea of theme and variation in music: If you can master it there are virtually no limits. Even if the contexts are not exactly the same: Tomáš Valena's[48] observations on type and topos seem relevant to me here. Topos refers to the characteristics defined by the culture, the site, the climate – the specific human capital. The task is to transform the type in such a way that it becomes appropriate to a concrete topos. **This is an interaction – between the ideal and the concrete. And, because it's**

---

48 Valena, Tomáš: Typos und Topos, in: Beziehungen. Über den Ortsbezug in der Architektur, e+s, Berlin 1994

an interaction, any attempt to address it from just one point of view is destined to fail.   And this is the most wonderful thing that I can experience, here and now, because it's this interaction that generates tension, life itself. This is not to be underestimated. As Mies van der Rohe stated, only intensity of life has intensity of form.[49]... And this, in turn, is about difference – about that special thing that I can distinguish. This gives us strength. And of course it's only made possible by its counterpart: indifference. This was an important word for Saint Ignatius on his retreats: It seems to have helped him to find the magnanimity and faith to put up with the state of the world; to accept the particularities of others; not to be too wrapped up in himself. It's precisely this that explains the coherence of a village such as Cons, the fact that Stefan – the neighbor who spends all his time chopping wood and working on his house, despite his advanced years – can make his door according to his own taste. Coher-

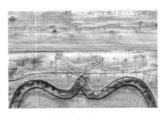

The door of Stefan's house.

ence comes from everyone being able to live life to the full.   **One could even ask: Can there be such a thing as type without variation?**   In any case that would produce bad monotony, barracks. And the results of variation without type can be seen on the edge of every town and village: diversity devoid of energy.

---

49 Mies van der Rohe, Ludwig: On Form in Architecture, 1927, transl. by Michael Bullock, in Conrads, Ulrich, Programmes and manifestos on 20th century architecture, MIT Press, Cambridge, Massachusetts 1971, p. 102.

Vernacular

You can't avoid it: The countryside is in vogue again. Congresses are being held and magazines devoted to the issue; Activities that used to belong in the country are becoming the hobbies of town dwellers – urban farming, for example. And the word vernacular is back in the architectural debate. We've heard it before – in England in the 1950s, in the USA in the 1930s.[50]   Isn't this exactly what postmodernism did? Look for new images. Of course the issue's been around for a long time thanks to, for example, the *Heimatschutz*, the early conservationist movement. But that movement was interested in more gentle images whereas the new vernacular is something grander, almost aggressive. Personally I find something questionable in even the notion of *Heimatschutz* as a search for authoritative images. Lucius Burkhardt says that the important thing is to protect not these images but their authors – those who created whatever it is that we want to preserve. Or, as the Japanese Haiku poet Basho says: Do not seek to follow in the footsteps of the wise. Seek what they sought.[51]   **Bruno Latour puts it similarly: "One is not born traditional; one chooses to become traditional by constant innovation. ... We cannot return to the past, to tradition, to repetition ... The idea of an identical repetition of the past and that of a radical rupture with any past are two symmetrical results of a single conception**

50 Basho, Matsuo, Words by a Brushwood Gate, 17th century, transl. unknown. Initially in England: Founded by "The vernacular architecture group"1952; for USA: Work by the pioneer Fred B. Kniffen in the mid-1930s; Fundamental: Bernard Rudofsky: anonymous architecture, 1983.

51 From the Haiku poet Bashô, quoted in Guzzoni, Ute: Das Wohnen und der Raum – Überlegungen im Ausgang vom Denken des späten Heidegger, Carinthia University of Applied Sciences, Spittal an der Drau 2014, p. 10.

of time."[52]   The past is fertile ground for the architect when interrogated from the present because then it can inspire us to look to the future. For me, discovering such potential would be a form of virtual perception. Tradition is based in the present, not only as described by Latour: It provides a sense of the loss of something valuable that's gone astray. And it's because of this that we start asking questions. I'm fairly sure that my grandfathers didn't know this feeling. They didn't speak of tradition, they experienced it. They had to act in the present whereas we can decide if we want to do so or not – a freedom that isn't always easy.

Crisis

Could one say: Tradition is a crisis – or evidence of the fact that the present is in crisis?   Is there such a thing as a relationship without a crisis? If there's no irritation, just consent and consensus, there's a threat of inertia. If we speak of an architecture of relationships then we must also speak of crises and ask ourselves how problems were addressed by earlier generations. That would be the tradition of innovation. Don't get me wrong. Consent is essential, unequivocal. But we obtain this consent when our answer to the crisis is to set things in motion. And the memory of this consent motivates these efforts; without it we would be helpless.   **Tradition and innovation are related. Innovation can only flout tradition by falling back on it – an interaction. In Latour's words it's about adding "to the never-ending refrain ... a sign, a shock, a shake-up, some small thing, some hint of something that comes from within**

---

52 Latour, Bruno: We have never been modern, transl. by Catherine Porter, Harvard University Press, Cambridge, Massachusetts 1993, p. 76.

it and puts its stamp of authority on the mundane phrase."[53]
This sheds a new light on the present – it's no longer "the attack on the rest of time," defined by Kluge.[54] Present: This is still the houses in which we live and the squares on which we meet – but not petrol stations and supermarkets; these are elusions. Our problems are here and now.   **In the words of Stephen Toulmin**[55]**: "The belief that, by cutting ourselves off from the inherited ideas of our cultures we can ... make a fresh start is ... illusory."**   But what if we can't stand these inherited ideas, the context? If it's all unbearable? If we have to escape? But we can't escape just like that. These inherited ideas cling to our heels. We only escape when we understand this relationship ... when we experience these ideas not as a monolith, but as events; when we notice the cracks and try to repair them through the power of change. Thumping the table: What's the point of that? But what about, as Latour said, "care, scruple, attention, contemplation, revival" and, I would add, cunning?   **Were the people of the mountains aware of this?** Were they aware? As long as they could leave the grand gestures to others, everything was fine. It was when they believed that they could also do this that the crisis began.

53 Latour, Bruno: Rejoicing: Or the Torments of Religious Speech, transl. by Julie Rose, Polity Press, Cambridge 2013, p. 78.

54 Kluge, Alexander: Der Angriff der Gegenwart auf die übrige Zeit, Syndikat/EVA, Frankfurt am Main 1985, transl. by R.H.

55 Toulmin, Stephen: Cosmopolis. The Hidden Agenda of Modernity, University of Chicago Press, Chicago 1990, p. 178.

Siat

One can talk about your work with knitted construction as an unfolding of the potential of this way of building. Starting from the layered or knitted corner joints with protruding timbers in the old farm buildings of Graubünden this process culminates in 2002 in the Mortuary in Vrin. Thereafter you vary the buildings with great skill, enriching them with new elements. But each year there's only one such building. New issues have arisen.   I never favor any constructional approach; it must fit the place and the function.

Interlocking and forming cells

One example is the guesthouse in Siat from 2011, a small, elegant establishment with a superior standard and multiple award-winning cuisine. Its architecture follows two principles

"Ustria Steila" Guesthouse, Siat, 2011.

with which you explain knitted construction: interlocking and forming cells. You can use these two terms to describe the entire building.   That's true in a number of ways. For one thing, today's wall has two or three layers in order to save energy. This isn't completely new: Buildings in Appenzell have a covering of shingles and buildings in Engadin one of stone. Here we can already see the difficulty: Shingles absorb settlement easily but in the case of stone one needs a different constructional solution. Then there's the dressing, the internal cladding that one finds, for example, in the parlors of the alpine uplands. The building in Siat has various combinations – two layers of knitting, knitting with an internal wooden cladding, internal wooden cladding with a plastered brick wall, a plastered brick wall with an external fair-faced concrete skin. There are several reasons for this – one being the fire regulations combined with the closeness of the neigh-bors. **That's the constructional aspect, another is the spatial one.** We gave this rather small building individual spaces; that's the cell principle. It applies to the entire upper level, the guest rooms, knit-ted – two-layered or with an internal clad-ding. This is evident on the outside, also quite expressively, due to the walls which protrude, purlin-like, from the façade. On the middle level each public room has its

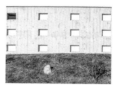

Detail of the façade of "Ustria Steila" Guest-house, Siat.

own character. Brick, plaster, and concrete dominate construc-tionally while wood is used atmospherically to establish the relationship with the guestrooms above. In the façade these public rooms step forward, white render between the wood of the upper level and the gray of the concrete base. ... This is perhaps the very opposite of systematic design. The building is composed as a series of spatial atmospheres, situational. Of course it's at the limit – or is it already too much? Has the building lost its autonomy? Is it too close to me, the user? If rigorous system building is at one end of a range of possi-bilities then this perhaps represents the other. **If knitted construction is defined by the terms cells and interlocking this suggests something iridescent, shimmering.** It's certainly not a pure system building like a timber-framed structure. It has a strict logic, but also plays with spatial atmospheres and pow-erful sensuality. This ambivalence forces one to behave – and opens up possibilities and, hence, combinations.

Connection and ornament

As one moves around and through the building there are constant associations with Carlo Scarpa.[56]   He was certainly highly individual, perhaps even emotional, and has to be taken seriously. In any case his work demonstrates a completely personal perception of space, quite unlike the systematic approach north of the Alps. On the one hand: a strong emphasis on sensual, material aspects; on the other: flowing transitions, overlaps, fewer sharp edges, relationships. **The cult of connection, of joining things in such a way that our joints – we know this since Semper – generate rhythmic structures and ornament.**   The building is an exercise in modeling with a range of materials, joining, connecting, twisting, decorating – not without logic. The most important room, the restaurant, makes its presence felt on the outside, without revealing itself completely, and is carefully detailed on the inside, has a wooden ceiling design with a central blue textile element that benefits the acoustics. Something that's often forgotten in restaurants.   **So, rather than being mere visual interior design, the room in which the guests eat was carefully considered in terms of their comfort.** These things that one can't see are very important to me. How are the acoustics of a dining room in the evening, of a ballroom, of a pilgrims' lounge? In the "Forest Hut" project we took this to an extreme: We wanted to create a silence in which one suddenly hears oneself, as one does when one's alone in the forest. If the creation of a space is focused on people, on

Carlo Scarpa, typical detail. Publication, Cologne 1994.

---

56 Scarpa, Carlo: Fondazione Querini Stampiala Venice, Mondadori Electa, Milan 2007.

the relationship between people and materials, then there's no other way. **Attention and acceptance, these are inescapable. Each of the public rooms in Siat has its own atmosphere. It's logical that this interconnected, open space is quite different.** This space is an active space. It has movement, people pass through, here's the counter, the buffet, there are also places to sit. This is an everyday room, a public room for the people of the village. Such a room is more robust, has a powerful timber-beamed ceiling, elongated proportions. It has a number of entrances and there's no calm center. The space is designed in line with the activities that happen within it, and reinforces them. ... But this also requires discipline. Space isn't defined by the user alone and the user certainly not by the space. Both are autonomous. This, and their relationship, must be balanced. **But one can pay too much attention; care can become welfare, caution protection. Architecture must resist this.** I certainly have my problems with autonomous architecture. But the same applies to the excessively anthropological approach, participation to the last drop. This underestimates the fact that it is things – things such as buildings – that initiate the actions of users. Which is precisely why they shouldn't be exclusively user-oriented. Both approaches are misleadingly exclusive and of no interest to me.

On the limit

This is a balancing act, and you're certainly testing the limits here. Yes, I can feel this. And I wouldn't take this any further right now. But it's important to test the limits. In the inn in Valendas the architecture is more distinctive. But that was also a different challenge: One is a public building, the other an almost private place of retreat. Different approaches are permitted.

Mastery – such as yours in the field of knitted construction – brings the danger of becoming affected. As long as you're aware of this, it's okay. But if you believe that you're the true master, then you'll develop no further. So: Be careful! And where's the tipping point? When the images begin to dominate, when one feels too much freedom, when the interdependencies – with the user, the place, the materials – are lost or taken too lightly. Be careful! In any case and above all: Stick with the space, beware of aesthetic exercises. Even if details are important to me: These must emerge, in line with the logic of the thing. **But that isn't an objection to the atmosphere of a space, to the challenge of designing it. It's just that one should strive to achieve this using spatial means.** Absolutely. And this demands far more energy and imagination than the retrospective design of interiors using colors and materials. The right choice of the appropriate atmosphere and the creation of this using spatial tools – these are elementary tasks right at the beginning of the design process. This is fundamental, and when one gets it right the furnishing can take care of itself. ... I'm sure that simple, knitted rooms are most appealing when things are placed freely within them – a Biedermeier chest, a baroque chair, a farmer's stool, a workbench. It's difficult when clients say: So, now I have to buy furniture that fits in. Fitting in is a bad basis for making architectural decisions. Good furniture fits in everywhere. Things shouldn't be able to get in the way of good architecture; they should simply be there – in a space that is simply good. **Which leaves open the potential for things to happen?** I guess so; I'm talking about spaces that are defined by qualities that inspire. I feel that neither the box of system architecture nor the aura of autonomous architecture is enough. I can't sleep well in a basement.   **An affinity with Joseph Frank comes to mind. His buildings, incunabula of classic modernism, have very individual spaces and he resolutely fought against the style of the day – New Objectivity – and the arrogance with which it sought to prescribe people's lives. And later he designed wonderfully playful, eccentric fabrics, furniture, and houses.**   Creating spaces for human life which don't tell people what to do but, rather, give them pleasure: This remains difficult. And, as soon as you believe that you've mastered it, it becomes even harder.

Beyond the limits

After working so intensively with knitted construction, after building for twenty-five years with wood, after your intense involvement with the village and your strong political commitment as a local councilor, the years around 2000 become a watershed moment. You step aside from your work for the village, from the valley, to a certain extent from knitted construction. We'd really reached the limit in terms of knitted construction – we were only able to realize the large windows of the school in Duvin with the help of a substructure. It was clear to me that I wanted to return to things that worked innately. A return that was a departure for pastures new. The Girls' Dormitory in Disentis, which we started designing in 2001, saw stone taking a decisive place in our oeuvre. Brick, lime, concrete. **Was the game over?** I still play – very seriously. We still create knitted construction; our approach to the rules is more confident, permissive. But our spectrum has broadened. My knitted construction comes from Vrin, it's more than construction; social and cultural aspects are important. This hasn't stopped.

A new game
And yet: You leave the pitch; the old game's over. Is a new one starting, a different one? One can also see the game from another perspective. Heidegger does this; he changes the

emphasis. He highlights the gamble, the risk, the jeopardy. Then the game is: taking life seriously, grasping unexpected opportunities, breaking habits, trying a different perspective – the cards are newly mixed. I take the leap which, in Heidegger's words, "as the most radical possibility of existence is capable of bringing what is most elevated to the clearing and lighting of being and its truth."[57] Disentis was something completely different – a big stone building. This was a leap into another reality; something new emerges. And so it was: A big change – most importantly for me.

Girls' Dormitory, Disentis, 2001–2004.

But you sense something: There are issues that say: Please don't go. This is always happening to me – I'm not a revolutionary. I'm always asking myself: Why don't I risk more, make a radical gesture? In my designs I try to get as far away as possible from reality, but the radical break: It's simply beyond me. I turn back ... **Can one turn back? Isn't one already heading in another direction? In his essay on the work of art[58] Heidegger defined art and design as the setting-itself-to-work of truth, by which he means: disclosing the essence of things. In other words: revealing the innate qualities of an object, giving them presence. In this sense, this act of disclosure, the great contribution of design, is about leaving-things-as-they-are. Such intellectual audacity! Rather than being**

57 Heidegger, Martin: The Principle of Reason, transl. by Reginald Lilly, Indiana University Press, Bloomington and Indianapolis 1996, p. 112.
58 Heidegger, Martin: The Origin of the Work of Art, transl. by Julian Young and Kenneth Hayes in Heidegger, Off the Beaten Track, Cambridge University Press, Cambridge 2002, p. 1ff.

something "new" the radical gesture becomes the act of revealing, disclosing, opening up, and releasing qualities that something already contains. This is the role of design. On the one hand it produces a world, enriches our human activity with things we've never seen before; and – according to Heidegger – it arranges the 'uncoerced' world of those things that it is beyond our ability to change.

Conflict

Heidegger considered these two activities – producing and arranging, the creation of the new and the revelation of the existing – as coming together, as being in opposition to each other, in the work, in the design. In other words: Design is conflict. Interpreted freely, this could mean that architecture is the confrontation between the unlimited possibilities of an idea and the relationship with a place. And the product of this search for equilibrium, this conflict, is architectural quality. It's this open-mindedness, this refusal to draw hasty conclusions as a means to an end that defines a work of art; and architecture can be part of this.   Design as an incitement to conflict – hmm, that sounds good. But a genuine conflict? Conflict is more than just dogmatism. This must be a particular sort of conflict. Opposition – and certainly not a legal dispute.   **Yes, not being rigid about something: a conflict, as Heidegger puts it, in which each reaches beyond himself.**   A struggle, a trial of strength, a contradiction, an interaction, a coming together – here material and place and people and discipline come into play in completely different ways. These have all been resonating since my watershed moment. All these voices are much closer and not so harmonious. If I look back it's really true: Initially, design was much more my responsibility, then some voices went quiet, but then others started up again and more things, even more people, joined in. Then one experiences trust, the trust of others, and so one trusts oneself more. ... Conflict, yes, this has its consequences. Earlier people came to me and saw me as a service provider who delivered what they ordered. But since I started involving, even making demands upon, my clients, their numbers have declined – not everyone likes that! It's a struggle, but it's worthwhile! **Objects are also sources of opposition – Valendas is an example. Two old buildings, one remains, one is to be replaced. How does one do this? Common approaches include more-or-less critical reconstruction or contrast, the celebrated joint. Your 'continuing to build in an almost identical way' is a different approach.** I simply carry on. Programmatic definitions help very little when you're wanting to play the game. Whether old or new, traditional or modern is of no interest. Only by freeing myself from these labels can I get to the point where interaction remains visible, opens up new possibilities. Producing something new that looks old makes as little sense as seeking to reinterpret the old as something new. 'Continuing to build' is much more pragmatic.

Valendas

So there's the old building in Valendas with all its constraints; a new one, with its own logic, is added. Between them: the stair. Here, this is much more than a rational-efficient method of changing levels. It's a link that belongs to both one and the other, as a result of which it's something in itself.

Meeting point of several stairs in "Gasthaus am Brunnen", Valendas, 2014. The stair connecting the old & new buildings meets the vertical circulation. The inn meets the open stair to the village hall.

Indeed, the first question was: Where do we put the stair? Then: What must the stair be able to do, where's the right position, for whom is it intended, what will it connect, does it belong to the building, to the square? For me something elementary can happen there: Someone climbs it from without, someone else descends it from within, they meet, unexpectedly, perhaps gladly, perhaps reluctantly. The stair plays the game of both buildings, it does more than fulfill a function, it's like an organ. I use it, but it can do more: Out, in, up, down, over there, back here and – I can reveal myself, I can conceal myself. This doing more, which is perhaps also a game, has become increasingly important to me. **Actually there's a threesome: Inn, old barn, square – public building, economy, village.** The population had a lengthy program. Square, public rooms, guest rooms, restaurant, (village) hall.

Street next to "Gasthaus am Brunnen", Valendas. The path within the building corresponds with the public path.

Today's wishes, old walls. Some remain, some don't. The barn's gone, its life is over. We removed every trace. We shouldn't chase old images. Old isn't better than new. Our new building has a strong relationship with the old inn and the buildings on the square: It's finished with lime. The key question: The square and the narrow streets – how can I reveal the new building in that setting, give it presence? Movement is important: how I climb the stair from the square, not at all obvious; what happens to the street; this is mirrored in the house – I can walk down the public street and see into the building; I can enter the building and see into the public street. And as a result the Bungert, the orchard behind the building, is enhanced, becomes a small public garden that relates to, extends, the small public room to the rear. Tangible events. **The street and the garden aren't images from a small town in an earlier, golden age but spaces where things happen. And if the building or any part of it continues to reveal the conflict between all that should happen here and what the situation allows, it comes alive.** I like to see a building less as an object and more as a partner. I'd love to have a building that lives with me. Not just that I live with the building but that it also lives with me. Let's take this space, the classroom of the school in Cons that I went to years ago with the oven at its heart. Here I regulate the temperature by moving – sometimes towards the oven, some-times towards the window. But if there's air conditioning why should I move at all? Or the window: What do the curtains do, or the shutters, how does the air get in, how do I look out? What is this brightness during the day, is it illumination, is it glare, what are these dark openings at night? I'd like to have a house that grows with me. That would be sensational! A house as a sounding board. **Perhaps the worst thing about building today is that we believe that a building is merely our instru-ment. That's so one-dimensional. The building that you long for serves you, but also challenges you, sets boundaries. A conflict between doing and 'leaving-things-as-they-are'. Such a building is both a challenge and something laid back, comfortable. As Heidegger says, it alters our usual perspective and gives us a jolt. It opens up the extraordinary and sweeps away the ordi-nary. It provides an impulse, a shove. This is how something new reveals itself.**

Event

You often talk about the event, especially in connection with the inn in Valendas. What do you mean by this? Take the question of design. What if a design doesn't just address this building, these spaces? What if questions come to the fore such as: What is this place? What happens here? People who participate, buildings that are here, things that happen – these influence the design as we understand it. Something happens that shapes the design, and the design itself happens. In Valendas, for example, the strong commitment of the people of the village, the meetings around the table in the inn that led to a different way of dealing with people and things. These gave me an insight into movements and relationships that were concretely reflected in the design – such as the unusual density of the stairs. **So an event refers to both a way of dealing with the building itself and something that precedes the building and the design.** That was the case. The people had intensely addressed the village and life in the village and the questions of how these were changing and what should happen in the future. That was a very good start! And it was clear to me that it needed a very good answer – a distinctive building. Less in the sense of an object dropped in from the outside but of something that expressed this strong commitment. Strong architecture can be created which transcends its location yet remains connected to it. This is how the autonomy of difference in different places is possible – or, put another way, something that stands out from the specific without following an abstract system. ... To achieve this I have to create some free space – cast off the limitation of ideas. This is where the active people of the village were so helpful. Experiencing this, being part of it, was a great release. They rose above the usual gossip in order to make this commitment to their village – this was extremely inspiring! And it was this that preceded the design, both chronologically and logically. It was fundamental. I could simply join in and take it to the next level. Distinctive architecture is less a product of social functions than of the momentum created by such shared liberation. The social and the autonomous, the traditional and the future-modern – these interact quite naturally. **Alain Badiou places the event at the heart of his thinking and says: "The event is something that enables a possibility to appear that was invisible or even unimaginable. ... In a certain way the event is only a suggestion. It suggests something to us. Everything depends upon the way in which this possibility is seized upon, processed, incorporated, and developed in the real world. This is precisely what I mean by a truth-process. ... The impact of this interruption in the real world, this interruption that is the event. ... The opening up of a possibility that wasn't predictable in advance."**[59] This was particularly explicit in Valendas but it can be applied to architecture in general. If everything in architecture is predefined then only that which you specify can happen. If, on the other hand, everything is completely open you wonder if anything will happen at all. People need something like guiderails. They're not very good with absolute freedom. ... The difficult question is, how much should be specified, defined? Can I act in such a way that the unpredictable is possible, that any possibilities remain open at all; that Badiou's events can occur? I find this game incredibly important. **Badiou emphasized that**

59 Badiou, Alain: Die Philosophie und das Ereignis, Turia + Kant, Vienna and Berlin 2012, p. 17, transl. from the German by R.H. Alain Badiou, *1937, French dramatist, mathematician and philosopher. Professor at the Université Paris VIII, Director of the Institute of Philosophy at the École normale supérieure. Still on his long march.

the event can't be planned.   But of course! That gives it something else, something erotic. Are we talking about a bolt of lightning? Hard work? Even if it comes out of the blue, it wants permanence.

Persistence

Unpredictable doesn't mean that something terribly secretive happens. In Valendas it was the moment when the village said: That's enough! That's completely understandable from the human perspective. One takes the initiative, doesn't allow oneself to be pushed around any longer. All of a sudden everything's different. This releases huge amounts of energy. One has to seize the opportunity: must allow oneself to be seized. This must be developed, taken further, achieve permanence. Badiou speaks of a "truth-process".[60]   If something happens to you then you must be ready to hand over control. And experience. This is interesting: give and take. Badiou says: "Action and inaction are more or less the same:"[61] Accept and act – I'm offered a choice and I decide.   **The architect is no longer the createur d'architecture. Another state of mind is important. "Being prepared for an event means being convinced that the world order, the dominating forces, aren't in absolute control."[62]**   Handing over control, being open to what happens, that's not easy for us. An old turn of phrase refers to 'being open to chance' in the sense of 'having an idea'. This

60 Badiou, Alain: Lob der Liebe, Passagen Verlag, Vienna 2015, p. 61, transl. from the German by R.H.

61 Badiou, Alain: Die Philosophie und das Ereignis, Turia + Kant, Vienna and Berlin 2012, p. 17, transl. from the German by R.H.

62 Badiou, Alain: Die Philosophie und das Ereignis, Turia + Kant, Vienna and Berlin 2012, p. 20, transl. from the German by R.H.

has been lost. But I maintain that this is another aspect of this profession that so readily presents itself as authoritative and controlled. We architects – unlike artists (as Loos made so clear to us) – have to deal with people; hence we have to be prepared for the unexpected. This is why architecture should be a sounding board. Not illustrate – resonate. ... A room in our Forest Hut was required for school classes, groups, even individuals, who have something to do in the forest or just enjoy being there. This had to be more than a mere container. The sensory aspects that are so important to children – warmth, smell, sound, feel – were also important to me: The building itself should stimulate feelings and sensations. Relationships should be activated because the things of the forest – in the forest – aren't what Bruno Latour called silent things. We wanted the hut to draw the secrets from the forest and one role of the architecture in this was to use constructional elements that would bring the forest into the building. Not just the material quality of wood, the diversity and richness of its surface, its many varieties, but also the density of the construction, its stockiness, the calmness of the space. This informed the design right down to the details. And during construction we sometimes had to resist temptation – such as that provided by the beautiful view of the countryside; instead of this we opened ourselves up completely to the forest.

Disentis

The event that begins with breaking with the customary manifests itself in the Girls' Dormitory in Disentis.   Something changed around 2000. Maybe it was a jolt. The stair in this building is an example; it's not a simple functional solution, more a collection of events. I get around the building, I can slip away, I encounter, experience space that creates time and place. And then it's not just the stair; it's the corridors that lead

Central stair in the Girls' Dormitory, Disentis. More than a functional space.

through the building, into the room, to the window. This can offer more than fresh air and views. We must free ourselves from the rules of the design manuals. Not that I'm saying that these are no longer valid. Of course rules about things like gradients, treads, and risers remain. Distancing, questioning doesn't mean that the rules don't remain very important – maybe they just have a new context. **The jolt of the design doesn't replace reality; it expands reality by altering the perspective.** Let me try to sum this up. To do this I must break it down, feel the elements, I detach myself from the whole, stumble upon contradictions that lead to new relationships. Transdisciplinarity describes this well – the skills of the individual disciplines aren't merged into one, they remain autonomous players. The same is true of a personal encounter: The other individual, the vis-à-vis, is essential, because otherwise there's no resonance. One must allow the elements of space and time to fuel this conflict, create energy. **Things aren't dead objects, separated from or beyond events, but have been created, have histories, have absorbed events. And only because of this are they able to return to becoming things that we can use, because they're able to open themselves to this, because they have the characteristic of the event.**[63] **What would we be able to make of something**

---

63 Badiou, Alain: Die Philosophie und das Ereignis, Turia + Kant, Vienna and Berlin 2012, p. 20, transl. from the German by R.H.

132

that lies dead at our feet? Ultimately I wouldn't be able to make anything of it at all. It needs a counterpart that's alive. Independent, capable of resonance, capable of the unexpected at any time. Something that surprises us – that happens to us, that's out of our control. If we keep our wits about us, a lot happens. Things that have an effect without me doing anything; dealing with these is exciting, dynamic. **Alive – something happens and I throw myself into it with heart and soul.** If I say that I design with all my senses, with sensory awareness, I'm speaking of the physical. This is more than my body, this is the time and space that I occupy, the body of my counterpart, his and my gestures. **This is obvious in spaces devoted to sociability, to hospitality – a focus of your design work in recent years.** I must move from the design to the space. As I cross this threshold interior design becomes interior creation. Interior design ties itself in knots because it's too narrow. Take restaurants for example: Here, gastronomic concepts are illustrated in terms of appropriate surfaces; then the guest is given a profile that should describe how he envisages a space and this is realized. The tautological circle keeps on turning – the interior designer: caught up in a looking glass war of images. Such spaces don't work, one doesn't want to remain in them, feels nothing in them, is trapped in a house of mirrors like at the fair. The staff anticipates your every wish and takes away your freedom. ... The same happens with places and buildings up here. Misguided architects convert our barns for people who have no relationship with the countryside and deceive these people into thinking that this is how we live up here. Colonialism through design. But no hill farmer, no housewife, ever lived in a barn. And then they want to buy it all. ... This is going on across the country – from small barns to whole resorts. But if I start with the living space, the space that I can fill with life through my actions, then I encounter other people, and they encounter me, properly, not as self-reflecting images.

Stair and square

This can be seen – or, better, felt – in the things that you make.

Observation tower in Goldau Nature Park, 2015. Two opposing stairs meet at the platform.

It's no coincidence that these are so often stairs. No surprise: This is where movement gains a truly spatial dimension. We've already spoken about Valendas; the tower in Goldau is another example. The tower is a stair or, more precisely, two stairs that enable the tower to stand, that rise, set up encounters. One could continue with the stair in the inn in Vals – a path that leads not up through but into the house, around the curve, takes the wall with it, and opens up before eventually meeting the old stair. Climbing stairs, up and back and forth, occupies the whole body, becomes an event – but don't worry: The building also has a lift! **Conversely one could say: This stair is kind to the body. It invites it to move, to experience the building – it develops in the space.** The stair relates and stores the memories that it teases out of those who are open to it. We become part of the story because things have stories. A good story says: beware. It helps. It entertains, it banishes boredom. **Has this become especially important in any project?** Yes, at the village square in Vrin with its new paving. The place where the villagers come together and confer is also a meeting place for spatial, material, and cultural energy – a complex network of streets, footpaths, tracks. It is in these flowing transitions that the village becomes comprehensible. When one says village square one says church. And that was built by Italians who came over the mountain just like the cattle used to be driven over the mountain in the other direction – my grandfather was such a cattle dealer. Antonio Beroggio, the architect from Roveredo, came in our direction. Everything of value came over the mountain. This shows how simple thinking can mislead: as if the head of a valley marks its end. That's where it begins! So my suggestion for the square was to perform this act again, to bring the stone from the south, pour life into this story. And that's what we did, brought the stone from there – not over the mountain but around it. Gneiss from the southern valleys, the nearby Bleniotal, something special that we don't have here. If that really interests the people of Vrin?

That doesn't matter – it's a story, I tell it and they tell it. ... We paved the square according to the customs of the villagers. Behavior becomes gestures – the square creates gestures. When one gets older one notices: The quality of life is the collection of stories. **Design is a gesture, not an idea. An idea is logically coherent, complete, final: A cube is a body consisting of identical, parallel edges and right angles. It couldn't be more perfect! The stair in the Hotel Alpina in Vals can't remotely be described in this way.** Because there's no such thing as finished, final, perfect in this world. The stair can't be anything other than unfinished because it's also shaped by the event of being used.

Paving of the village square, Vrin. The stones adapt to the terrain and lead to every front door.

Time

In this sense the term perfection is inadequate. Because it often happens quite differently; you sit together with people, talk about a project, want to find the solution to a problem, but it simply can't be found. Then you go home and suddenly it's there, the flash of inspiration. I don't know exactly how it happens, it can't be explained. The will is there, but the solution appears to come from a completely different direction. But then I'm suspicious of this flash, I want to destroy it, fight with it. Can I trust it? Isn't it experience that leads to new knowledge? **Human thought isn't just the sequential processing of information but what Ernst Pöppel called "massive parallelism". It can be shown that this neurological activity is particularly intense when we're young but that when we're older and this activity is somewhat reduced we compensate by resorting to tried and tested approaches. You could call this the neurological background of experience.** I also feel this when I'm working with students. One could conclude from this that at every age, at every moment, one should do what one does best. A viable society must be prepared to make use of this range of abilities rather than just worshipping youth, speed, perfection. ... I experience things up here, every inhabitant of Vrin knows them, that are so beyond time, beyond space. Is it still day or is the night already falling, are the clouds above me or around me, is that rain from above or moisture coming from the meadow, is the green turning to gray or the gray turning to green? Is it time-space or space-time? What is this measuring of time, this pigeonholing? **Is this form of "rational" really so timeless?** Acceleration and efficiency count. The quick result is preferred over sustainable quality, it promises one thing above all others: instant returns. **Whereas you speak about**

experiences that come from another age.   The ideas come faster, intuition is easier; it's like this weather: uncertain, with a relaxed intensity, like I experienced when playing football. Have I become more relaxed, more open, inclined to the unexpected?

Chance
"Over all things stands the Heaven Accident, the Heaven Innocence, the Heaven Contingency, the Heaven Exuberance," says Nietzsche through the lips of Zarathustra.[64]   Yes, childish exuberance evokes happenings, events. And if we don't work everything out to the last detail, perhaps we even gain a brief glimpse of this innocence. ...   **It's not much different in real life. We also talk about planning our lives; but if I look back I have to say that chance played more of a role.**   But intention and chance go together. If I look back at how I sought to leave the valley then this required a strong will. One wants to leave the nest, go out into the world, leave tracks. One can't tolerate chance events. Experience comes from intention. It doesn't just happen, I must also be ready for it. It has to be challenged, provoked. And this can also hurt. In any event it's not the easy path that leads to every experience. Only with time is one aware of one's own failure; of the fact that this is part of the journey. But are such moments completely lost? It seems as if something's retained, like in an archive, from time to time we take something in – but it can't be planned.   **One can't force chance to happen, at best one can create the necessary conditions.**   And if something like this happens, if I'm unsure if

64 Nietzsche, Friedrich: Thus Spoke Zarathustra, transl. by Graham Parkes, OUP, Oxford 2005, p. 143.

it's good or not, then the whole thing starts again: Check very carefully, examine from a range of perspectives and: the belief, that's good, stick with it, work hard, until you drop, with maximum intensity. And then finally – now it's right. Giacometti described it like that. **That's so hard to understand in an age so fixated upon precision and efficiency. Few in our profession were capable of it – The Viennese architect Josef Frank was one of them. He was convinced about chance, put perfection in its place and even created a word for the process: 'accidentism'.[65] This sounds like "accident". Not just chance but accident. Frank had lived too long in America not to know this. In our perfectly planned world there's no such thing, because it's not permitted. Frank knew better – and had some confidence in it. His skepticism about reason had yet another side: He rehabilitated the sentimental. One should let people have their longings, not sacrifice everything to the tin gods of objectivity. His maxim: design the context as if it all occurred by chance.** Of course that's asking a lot. It reminds me of what some people say about my buildings, that they look as if they've always been there. I have real problems with this. It's as if it's all childsplay, a little unplanned. **Although Frank knew this: "Nobody feels comfortable in an ordered environment that is forced on them ... We long for streets that are something other than simply traffic problems, however neatly solved they may be."[66]** Architecture is more than just the solution to a problem.

65 Frank, Josef: Akzidentismus (1958), transl. by Ruth Kvarnström-Jones, in: Mikael Bergquist & Olof Michelsen: Accidentism, Josef Frank, Birkhäuser, Basel 2016. Josef Frank, Austrian architect, designer and visionary, one of the leading figures of the modern movement as well as one of its first critics.

66 Frank, Josef: Akzidentismus (1958), transl. by Ruth Kvarnström-Jones, in: Mikael Bergquist & Olof Michelsen: Accidentism, Josef Frank, Birkhäuser, Basel 2016, pp. 23 and 24.

Or do we simply have to reinvent function? In the way, for example, suggested by Goethe: "existence, expressing itself through form, can be seen in living, relative function."[67] How does a person feel, how does he move, what troubles him, what pleases him? Given that people are different there's no conclusive answer. Yet we still try to satisfy everyone. If it's too open there's no social contact; if it's too narrow nothing happens. I'd be surprised if chance wasn't partly responsible for this unstable equilibrium.

In vain

Event, chance – This is what happens if "the world order doesn't have complete control." The unexpected, incalculable, different happens – Badiou calls this otherness. "The difference, the otherness, is my starting point."[68] That suits your preferences. And it's obvious that it isn't abstract. "There are no world events. There are events around the world. There are local constraints."[69] I see it like this: If you don't concentrate on the place you won't find any examples of chance, perhaps there aren't any. Chance is something special; it resists generalization. It's the same with buildings. The precision of a timber-framed building leaves nothing open to chance – unlike knitted construction with its settlement and living cracks. The presence of wood as a living material is open to chance – but in timber-frame buildings this tends to disappear below

67 Goethe, Johann Wolfgang: Naturwissenschaftliche Schriften, Vol 10, Böhlau, Frankfurt 1897, English version Ute Poerschke, Architectural Theory of Modernism, Routledge, London, p. 12.

68 Badiou, Alain: Die Philosophie und das Ereignis, Turia + Kant, Vienna and Berlin 2012, p. 68f, transl. from the German by R.H.

69 Badiou, Alain: Die Philosophie und das Ereignis, Turia + Kant, Vienna and Berlin 2012, p. 140, transl. from the German by R.H.

synthetic cladding. I'm convinced that one can design architecture that's open to chance and events. Without events, chance becomes pure orchestration. **Designing architecture that permits chance: that's a challenge. How should it work?** There's not a single order, there are hierarchies of order, overlapping structures. Take Disentis, for example: There you have the volume with its massive order, the levels, entrances in alternating directions, on the outside just one visible at a time, on the inside a complex tangle which becomes playful, light. One can see: the game of clarity and diversity, even ambiguity. ... Or in Valendas: There you have this space next to the large room, its stage. If I close the wall and enter it from the other side it's a library, an ancillary space. If I turn round and open the window it's the loggia, almost dominates the square. A pivot, heterotrophic, a space which flows when used, ambivalent; functionally imperfect, its qualities emerging from its interaction with the neighboring space, the space it serves. Another example in the same building: A column stands in the center of the public room of the inn. How can this happen? It's in the way, right in the middle of the

Intermediate space in "Gasthaus am Brunnen", Valendas. The column organizes the space, defining sub-spaces.

room, annoying. It wouldn't have been hard to find a structural solution and remove it. But it stayed, and now it's doing something. But what? A large room, clearly laid out, similar sides, in which one prefers to stand against the wall. But now I have to move to see everything on the other side, have to avoid the column to get to the other side, different areas emerge, regular tables for women and men. This column stimulates moments of uncertainty. Crises? Reactions at least. The not quite perfect triggers the unexpected. **One occasionally comes across people who are very precise in their work and yet have a fine sense of this connection; I read, for example, in a work by a novelist who's seen as very severe: "Yet everything of price falls to us by chance; the best is unpaid for."[70] Ernst Jünger confirmed this.** Wonderful. Let's build lots more 'of price'! What a wonderful phrase that would be for architects. Joseph Frank would definitely have agreed. There are certain similarities with the work of his contemporary and compatriot Bernard Rudofsky. Is it a surprise that he became famous through his exhibition "Architecture without Architects"?[71]

Luck

Rudofsky argues that effective everyday objects should be left alone. It's remarkable how many of his examples come from the Mediterranean. Is this region more conducive than ours to the virtue to which Rudofsky is referring: Serenity? Which isn't far removed from something else that our profession doesn't like to acknowledge: Luck. I know how difficult design can be. It's got better over the years, become somewhat less intense, and I find it easier to say: It's a success. This is good; you need serenity to be able to allow luck to play a role in the design process. **Ernst Jünger again: "If the dice rolls for us, the page turns for us, we experience an exquisite pleasure – the pleasure of a secret, material intelligence. In truth, luck is nothing more than the elementary form of intelligence – when we're lucky, the**

70 Jünger, Ernst: On the Marble Cliffs, transl. by Stuart Hood, Penguin, London 1970, p. 28.
71 Rossi, Ugo: Bernard Rudolfsky, architect, Napoli 2016.

things, the world are thinking for us."[72] Does one have to be a poet to say this? That success is a result of things, the world, thinking for us! The material intelligence of things acting on our behalf.   But I must stick with them, trust in their ability to do something, trust myself. Have confidence in what happens, let it happen ... In a current project we're having to insert a new building into old built fabric. There was this thick, ancient wall against which we wanted to build the circulation core, flush, without any steps in the wall. Then it became clear that the old wall was no longer structurally sound: The new, replacement wall was much more slender so suddenly we had something new, a niche, that enriched the adjacent room with its smooth walls, gave it more quality. It's clear that we didn't come up with this – the dilapidated old wall had done the thinking for us. That was such a stroke of luck. This happens. Things have something to offer us. Of course we have to be open to it, to recognize it. This comes with time, requires experience. Trusting to luck, recognizing and accepting the enrichment that it can bring – I can put it like this: The thing thought on my behalf. I've never felt the potential of refurbishment as much as I have in this project – time and space brought together by looking backwards and looking forwards.

---

72 Jünger, Ernst: Das Abenteuerliche Herz, Munich 1997, p. 83, transl. by R.H.

Vella

Alongside such out-of-the-ordinary projects as a dairy, a forest hut, and two towers, other buildings realized over the course of the past fifteen years play a prominent role in their context. Big buildings, massive volumes, of stone – the Girls' Dormitory in Disentis, the inns in Valendas and Vals. Most recently a new building in Vella.

Large volumes

A mixed-use building in one of the main villages in Val Lumnezia, a large building for the region given its dimensions of around 15 x 20 x 12 meters. A shop on the ground floor, doctors' surgeries on the first, apartments above. It was during planning discussions with the municipality that apartments were added to the large roofspace, also in order to give the building presence. The interest in large, resolute volumes became clear. The newcomer should rank with the most important buildings in the village –

a small, late renaissance castle, an imposing post office of the early *Heimatschutz* movement, a large, mid-twentieth-century inn …

Grand buildings to which the municipality is now adding another.

Vella. Large buildings shape the heart of the village.

Even up here it's important to understand what makes a place unique. In Vella this is the rhythm of small and large buildings – quite unlike Vrin, which appears as a series of identical structures; or Malans, where the variety is much more radical. Vella's few large buildings are integrated in a balanced way. They have meaning.

The municipality wanted the same from a building with doctors' surgeries and a large shop. These buildings are close

Mixed-use building in Vella, 2016.
Symmetry characteristic to the village.

to the road but, rather than being parallel to it, they're perpendicular, facing it with their gables. They have a direction, a pitched roof – a design tool that a cube doesn't have. **You can no longer use knitted construction at this scale?** That's the first thing. But I also wanted my large, imposing building to be massive, stone-like, as is the custom up here. Knitted construction, cellular building, is also incompatible with the sought-after spatial structure of large, flexible volumes and didn't come into question in this location. In contrast, all of Vella's farmhouses, cowsheds, and barns use knitted construction. Their volume, function, and constructional method reflect their social significance. This is often a problem today: A certain appearance is preferred and little attention is paid to the nature of a structure.

Hybrid

The relationship between volume and constructional method in Disentis is similar but, unlike the compact method used there, the building in Vella had to have an open plan. A further step becomes necessary: The switch from a wooden to a stone cell structure is followed by the switch from the stone cell to the stone open-plan space. This has structural consequences – it becomes a hybrid building. It's a timber building clad with stone. Assuming that one wants to avoid synthetic materials it's harder to insulate stone buildings than timber ones. The options are a highly complex double-skin construction, a composite system with external insulation or internal insulation that has to be vaporproof. This is a disaster for the indoor climate. Much better products are available if you build with timber. You can use renewable and breathable materials. We wanted both. **A wooden casket placed in a stone cloak?** The opposite! The wood supports the stone. It's a timber structure, load-bearing timber posts, columns, and beams (with the exception of the steel columns in the shop) supporting a 12.5 cm external brick wall. The stone is actually a covering. **And then there are the floor slabs which are also hybrid structures.** Yes, this is a composite timber-concrete solution. The reason: I have to think about not only the structure but also the sound insulation. This requires mass. The functional and spatial character is closer to that of an industrial space than of a barn. This enables us to have a free and flexible plan. But we don't know how the use will develop. **Now such a hybrid is somewhat impure in the sense of material unity – perhaps also in the sense of your earlier beliefs.** Earlier I would've said: I won't do that, it's not honest! But one has to admit that even the earlier farmhouses weren't that pure. They were also clad, often with several layers. The stone houses of Engadin have timber on the inside. ... Today there's a new wave: homogenous structures of, for example, insulating concrete. These are fascinating, but they also use mixtures; in the concrete: additives, then steel and cement. And the solution that looks so convincing in the laboratory as a free-standing outside wall looks quite different in reality when I have to connect the slab or build in a window. ... Earlier I was convinced by pure construction, in awe of the one and only truth; today, I see truth completely differently. Mixed construction is nothing new; we've always sought the best available solution for pragmatic reasons. This is also a risk, also demands serenity. But the material must always have something to do with the place. We work with materials that are found locally and with which local craftspeople can work. Relationships emerge, with the people and with the things. Something's happening! The choice of materials is a cultural undertaking that has ecological and economic consequences for a place.

Mixtures

Such a structure is actually a practical example of the dubious nature of pure doctrine. It's good to see how dependent things are upon each other. This becomes very clear in the expansion of the hut on the Greina. This also has wood – inside. In this treeless landscape at an altitude of 2,200 meters the warmth of wood has a special authority. This is a solid

Haus Terri, Greina, 2008. Wood wrapped in stone.

timber building, 14-cm-thick, laminated panels. On the other hand: Wood is quite unsuitable for exposure to such climatic and weather conditions. So we wrapped the wood with stone in the tradition of the alpine hut. The Greina has stone, water, the horizon – and nothing else. Stones were gathered *in situ* and transformed into a 30-cm-thick masonry wall – but without the wooden core this wouldn't have worked. **This means that these two buildings owe their existence to an analogous principle: the conflict between contradictory subjects.** Timber building/stone building, warm/hard, the traditionally designed mountain hut or town house/new ideas. If one considers these questions, one

146

sees this slightly differently. Just like the way in which we used tradition logically when building the hut, we did the same in Vella: We took the traditional built hierarchy further. **Also by adopting the defined order and symmetry that large buildings have been developing since the Renaissance. There's a base with a public use, a bel étage for the doctors, and the apartments under the roof. The classic horizontal organization of a town house.** But be careful: That's the urban perspective. Look at the barns up here and you'll see the same thing: A stone base, then a rectangle of knitted timber, topped off by an open structure of round logs. That's the farmer's perspective. **Okay, two ways of seeing a single phenomenon, the structured façade. In any case the townsfolk shopped on the ground floor, lived nobly on the first floor and resided simply above. If we turn to the other direction, the vertical, it remains classical: central axis and symmetry.** The free façade certainly has its appeal and its justification – the alpine hut is like this, and the dairy in Disentis, too. But then I also discovered the appeal of symmetry. Symmetry is naturally compelling in itself. **This is largely due to the position of the typology in the constructional hierarchy, this makes it compelling. A building is derived from its urban context. First the location, then the function.** I'd say: both are of equal importance. And then something strange happens. In the floor with the doctors' surgeries there's a strict series of closed and open walls – precisely where flexible spaces were required. And we realized the extent to which rigor and flexibility are compatible. This is why it's a fallacy to believe that a free plan requires a façade made up of vertical posts that offer any number of options for connecting internal walls. **Symmetry, rhythm, proportion – it's these that offer freedom. Classical buildings built in line with these principles**

guarantee the amount of freedom required by users; anything more is an exaggeration. Are we too strict? Isn't the hybrid an answer to this? This rejects doctrine. Holding on to a single truth that's written in stone requires enormous effort. This search for homogeneity is actually out of place in architecture, which is about developing credible solutions that reflect both objectives and possibilities. The pragmatic approach of the hybrid is a solution that's crying out to be mastered; the pure solution on the other hand is a source of unnecessary stress.

Plasticity

Architecture is always a potential answer, not a definitive truth; flexibility is required. The Girls' Dormitory in Disentis displays this in a surprising way. Integrated into the heart of the village of Disentis and yet unusual due to its mass, this authentic, powerful cube which is built into the hillside is apparently seeking to support the enormous abbey complex above. And they are, indeed, related. The girls, each of whom lives in her own room down here, go to school up there. The building appears regular but there are differences within and between the façades, a feature that emphasizes the liveliness of the volume. The dominant impression is one of mass and plasticity. This was already an issue in knitted construction, for that has a plasticity that results from how it's made; the wall wraps around the corner, openings are created in this wall, etc. ... Plasticity isn't an add-on. This is also true of Disentis where it may have more to do with the use. The fixed glazing of the larger windows is flush with the outside wall so that the deep sill becomes a window seat whereas the smaller opening light is flush with the inside wall and the external stone sill advances a few centimeters beyond the plastered façade; this game generates relief and rhythm across the entire wall. Even the fixed windows are plastic in themselves. Being flush they require special protection; this is the job of a separate auxiliary frame that ensures that the glass surface sits deeper than usual. These are the small building blocks of plastic design. Today I'd love to take this approach further. **The plasticity is also a result of the urban setting – on the one hand! On the other hand: of the window seat.** Plasticity must emerge from the building as a whole. The spatial structure – a series of identical living cells – suits the regular façade essential to the urban situation. But this is interrupted in two places: by the unaligned window of the communal space and a much larger one that opens onto the loggia. This is in a different position on each side of the building. The result is plasticity. But, like decoration, this is only credible when it's derived from the life of the building. Only this can stop it becoming pretentious, arbitrary, short-lived individualism.

Window of the Girls' Dormitory, Disentis. The plasticity of the building reappears at the window, adding to the life of the user.

Delicate mass

This cube gives the impression that more cubes are stacked within it. Perhaps due to the cube-shaped windows? Yes, each room is a cell in the large cube and then there's this loggia at each level that introduces a little leeway, slightly relaxes the rigorous structure. And this loggia then becomes part of the communal space. We've observed how the girls take possession of this space and feel disturbed when strangers enter it. This has something to do with the heart of the building which is also the heart of one of these communal spaces: a plastic staircase with a quiet niche and a kitchenette. This is the nest that we've built, in concrete which has the same color as the valley. **It's remarkable what this heart offers: kitchen, quiet area, cozy corner, lift, stair – all as a spatial experience.** One should also include the accesses to the various levels. The

Central stair of the Girls' Dormitory, Disentis. Enhanced use and form thanks to the well-thought-out circulation within the building.

sloping site allowed each to be entered directly. This means that, rather than having to be an enclosed fire escape, the stair can be a living space that's experienced at every level. And the steps and their underside can become a spatial element. Now I can move easily between the levels, emerge, conceal myself. With the result that spatial structure, function, activity, and plastic design become one. **The different orientation of these communal spaces towards the four points of the compass is also related to the entrances and the topography.** These spaces are organized according to the same principles yet each is different. On one level this is a morning space, on another a space that comes into its own at midday, etc. The living cells are developed in the same way. Small units, designed with care, down to the last spatial detail. The shower partition, for example, becomes a seat when the curtain is drawn back. The building reacts delicately to being used by such tender creatures. A boys' dormitory might look completely different. **Delicacy and mass – are these compatible? Shouldn't buildings for young people be light and slender and buildings for the powerful heavy and unresponsive? Or is it the complete opposite: Doesn't delicacy flourish much better**

in massive, almost rough, surroundings? That's right, delicacy has nothing to do with dimension. A thick column can be so delicate! The question is: How is it positioned in the space, in which space? **A detail. An entrance, a stair leads upwards, disappears into the wall. The stair begins far from the cube. It climbs five steps before reaching the façade and disappearing through a high opening. A transition, impressively clear and simple and yet still surprising.** That's the key. It's the transitions, the interactions, that bring life. Mass, not as a principle but as a contrast. That's how things should develop. **Interaction: This leads to a variety of solutions – One of Badiou's favorite words and one with consequences. "The objective existence of variety brings ... the possibility that something unexpected happens that can be neither predicted nor calculated."[73] He continues: "And given that my thinking includes the notion of chance, it isn't deterministic."[74]** This is familiar to us: conversations in which your sentence is answered by a no and, when you dig deeper, by the next no. Yes, yes, no, no. Soul-destroying. But the comparative form is actually no more than: Yes, but ... Conversely, however, there's a conversation in which I say something that you pick up on and slightly change by subtly twisting it before I pick up on this and gently reverse it again. It's as if the truth is going on a journey. A journey that can last for hours. An intellectual ramble that, like a real ramble, never takes the shortest route between two points. Something else is happening here. This has nothing to do with drawing quick conclusions, rather with developing possibilities.

---

73 Badiou, Alain: Die Philosophie und das Ereignis, Turia + Kant, Vienna and Berlin 2012, p. 139, transl. from the German by R.H.

74 Badiou, Alain: Die Philosophie und das Ereignis, Turia + Kant, Vienna and Berlin 2012, p. 142, transl. from the German by R.H.

As Kluge put it, "I'm interested in the potential solutions rather than the truth."[75] Or, as my ETH colleague Michael Hampe (77a) once advised: Don't suggest; report!

---

75 Von Schirach, Ferdinand und Kluge, Alexander: Die Herzlichkeit der Vernunft, Luchterhand, Munich 2017, p. 126, transl. by R.H.

Production conditions

How do we make architecture today? The highlights in the media are the work of big companies with hundreds of employees, offices all over the world, special departments, competition teams, and creative staff. They design incessantly, pass on the buildings for execution when they're successful and, if not, register, document, archive, save them so that they're always available. Nothing's wasted, everything's used. Data processing ensures access to everything, from everywhere, at any time.

I remain dependent upon my own experience; I must assimilate the alien, working alone; see how I respond to it from within. This is me and this is the world, this is how it is, here and now at least, unique.

Intensity

Your production conditions: three or four employees, an office of, maybe, 20 square meters, a workshop, 1,440 cubic centimeters of brainpower; plus the mountain air, the valley, the village, the family, and, for some time now, your professorship.   More input wouldn't allow me to gather experience in the way I need it. Information, information processing isn't the sort of know-how that I work with. I must experience, deepen this experience, discover forms of original experience. To

Workplace: Caminada's studio.

experience is to live and this also has something to do with the experience of the end, for it's this that gives life its special quality, its uniqueness – it isn't infinite, available at will, permanently accessible. This may be true of machines; but this means that the machine can't have the experience that I have, that I'm dependent upon. Is this a deficit, an asset? In any case it's something else.   **Isn't this experience of the finite a precondition for the experience of intensity?**   The physical, walking, working – these draw me to things, put me in awe of them. An awe that can also be about enduring something, especially up here. It's about living, not building. About feeling alive. That's the only way I can envisage intensity.   **The architect Franz Riepl said that quality can only result from intensity.**[76]   Or, put another way, intensity leads to a different sort of architectural quality, one that isn't about fulfilling a brief, completing tasks. **Mies van der Rohe linked intensity of life with intensity of form.** He would have known – and was able to sum it up so simply. Impressive!

Walking

Intensity of life, this means being aware of the senses, of the body. What would become of us thinking beings without awareness and action and, decisively, hands and legs, those very special organs of the bodily space? This is particularly true up here.   Quite right, we were always in motion, on our feet, on foot, wherever we were we had to take our place, stand firm, stand on our own two feet, keep our feet on the ground, act correctly in the sense of: What's coming up and how

---

76 Riepl, Franz: Das entsteht nur in der Intensität, in: Florian Aicher u. a. im Gespräch – Bauen in Bayern, Callwey, Munich 1996, p. 73 ff.

should we deal with it? The landscape forced you to take a stance. **An aphorism of Emil Cioran emphasizes the liberating effect of thinking out in the open.**[77] **You must be aware of this – below the open sky, on the move, mountains on the horizon. Is it easier to think outdoors?** Perhaps it's best at high altitude. When I'm out walking the ideas come more easily, they flow, but they also slip away, I have to take care to retain them, I often want to write them down. But eventually they return. ... It's different in the church. The ideas turn up while you're standing there. I'm still aware of them two days later. But they don't flow. ... **Apparently Kierkegaard said that he walked to his best ideas. And Ernst Bloch's**[78] **metaphor for dignity, independence, and the inalienable rights of man is that if one doesn't open oneself up, one can't walk upright. The upright posture comes as a result of walking. Man isn't grounded like a tree by its roots. He finds balance through movement.** We're stable when we walk, I can withstand a gust of wind when I'm in motion. Our root is our movement in space, in time, in our head. I experience the topography of the mountains by moving. Standing still is strenuous, tiring, cuts off several potential solutions. Movement is a source of pleasure and hope. **Stability and motion – the legs are capable of both. They define your life from childhood onwards, define your place; this isn't an object, it's your leg, your hand, your head. And that's why this place isn't something detached, mysterious, it's your life, your work. It's been given to you.** This place is inexhaustible, even if the possibilities aren't unlimited; indeed, the possibilities up here are severely

77 Cioran, Emil M.: Gevierteilt, Frankfurt 1982, p. 100.
78 Bloch, Ernst: Naturrecht und menschliche Würde, Suhrkamp, Frankfurt 1972, p. 12.

limited. There's this plank – just this plank; what can I make out of it? How the idea of *creatio ex nihilo* would amaze the people up here, make them laugh! There isn't much up here, not much distraction, not much entertainment, it's boring, one has to work harder, deal with things, make something of them. **The place demands something of you, forces you to focus. This creates a wealth of experience, intensity, intuition. Daniel Humm, a compatriot of yours who was named the world's best chef in 2017, created this intensity in the same way. Take the first steps, become better intuitively, want to know more and then it happens: a dish. "That changed my life." This was something basic that reached back to his childhood and had guided him ever since: "We want to understand how it was back then. We want to get back to this feeling of pure creativity."[79]** Isn't this the key thing about design: this sense of clarity of what something is really about? This is based on experience, experience with which I, naturally, wrestle, that I scratch away at until I find something that I can hold onto.

The threshold

You're describing a sort of primeval experience. You're speaking of the threshold. Not an abstract one, any old threshold, but the threshold to the barn. The threshold to the barn is high, around 30 cm. But the free height of the door is only about 140 cm. This point of transition between outside and inside, between inside and outside is a special place. I spent a lot of time here as a boy, alone, with my father or with my siblings.

---

79 Humm, Daniel: Sellerie hat mein Leben verändert, in: SZ 21.7.2017 Samstagsküche, transl. by R.H.

We played and scratched symbols in the wood with pocket knives. As soon as the cows came we had to leave. The animals stopped in front of the threshold, stood rigid, motionless for a moment, looking at us with their huge eyes. Sometimes when snow had fallen in summer they'd been driven down a long way from the top of the mountain and were suddenly standing there at the threshold staring at

The origin: the threshold.

me, hungry and steaming. Huge eyes, longing to enter. The eyes of a cow – greatest wisdom, boundless simplicity – it's all there. And then, with a swift movement, they lifted their hooves and effortlessly crossed the threshold to the inside. This physical movement was a ritual. As well as being the location for such diverse events, the threshold also controlled these events as they occurred and provided the boundary between different atmospheres. In bad weather it was a climatic divide. The space provided shade, offered protection against heat and rain. The threshold divided not only temperatures, but also odors, into zones. I always enjoy returning to this place. The threshold's still there where it always was. But the cows cross it no longer. The patina of age and the shrinking and swelling of the wood have rendered the symbols and scratches of our pocket knives all but unrecognizable. Now there's something mystical about them.

The eyes of the cow

Has this experience faded together with the threshold? The memory of this lost way of life is still awake. I can build upon it. A part of that which was irrevocably condemned to death returns to life. Is this transcendence? For me, the memories of this threshold become a manifesto for relationships, for precise, careful observation, for a world beyond nature and culture, for their values and unassuming wealth. The threshold has a physical and a spiritual form and speaks of events that have happened, good and less good. It seems to record life in all its many aspects. If I leave beside my memories and remain in the present I tend to see the threshold as a metaphor for holistic architecture. For an architecture that incorporates space, topography, material, and construction in the same way that it incorporates the uniqueness of the object and the related emotions and events that enrich the object through the possibilities that they bring, past, present and future; that connect us with those that came before and are with us now; that create a – rich – day-to-day existence that makes the act of creation worthwhile. A day-to-day existence that demands retrospection and revolution. That is how it could emerge, this architecture that I long for.

The fact that design ideas flow more easily with time: Does this have something to do with the fact that this original experience is so present, that it first had to become present? Speaking for myself, yes. Whether this is true for others is hardly relevant. Things must firstly stand on their own. ... I believe that it's this that makes a design credible. This is my contribution to this world and it's unlike the neutral product of the machine. The rationality of the machine isn't enough. Experience, action, reflection are required. Experience and thinking have to complement each other in the form of reflection. Not as theories, those "over-hasty efforts of an impatient understanding that would gladly be rid of phenomena,"[80] as Goethe once put it.

---

80 Goethe, Johann Wolfgang: Maxims and Reflections, transl. by T. Bailey Saunders, Macmillan, London 1906, p. 184.

The work of design is to work with experience. I'll always return to my precious threshold, the repository of my childhood memories. It contains secrets and hopes, it is reality and utopia. It reveals things that I alone understand because they belong to me. It enables me to see the world – through these wonderful eyes of a cow.

Gion A. Caminada and Florian Aicher

The participants

Gion A. Caminada, architect and professor at the ETH,
   *1957 in Vrin, CH
Florian Aicher, architect and author, *1954 in Ulm, D
Francois Burkhardt, design theorist, *1936 in
   Winterthur, CH
Petra Steiner, photographer, *1967 in Saalfelden, A

I have been following this path for a long time.
And my thanks are due to all those who have accompa-
   nied me.
In particular I have to thank my wife Giuseppa, who has
enabled me to do so much. Who has allowed me the freedom and given me the energy to set forth, time after time.
Gion A. Caminada